Cover

Popular fiction series

Series Editors: Tony Bennett   and Graham Martin
               Associate Professor,   Professor of English
               School of Humanities, Literature, Open
               Griffith University   University

First in the series:

Cover Stories
Narrative and ideology in the British spy thriller
by Michael Denning

Forthcoming:

Memory Making
The representation of the period 1918–1945 in
contemporary popular writings
by Roger Bromley

Popular Fiction
Technology, ideology, production, reading
A Reader edited by Tony Bennett

Popular Film and TV Comedy
by Steve Neale and Frank Krupnik

Also forthcoming:

John Caughie on Television Drama

Colin Mercer on Popular Narrative

Popular Fiction Series

Cover Stories

Narrative and ideology in the British spy thriller

Michael Denning

Routledge & Kegan Paul
London and New York

First published in 1987 by
Routledge & Kegan Paul Ltd
11 New Fetter Lane, London EC4P 4EE

Published in the USA by
Routledge & Kegan Paul Inc.
in association with Methuen Inc.
29 West 35th Street, New York, NY 10001

Set in 11 on 12 pt Sabon
by Inforum Ltd, Portsmouth
and printed in Great Britain by
The Guernsey Press Co. Ltd,
Guernsey, Channel Islands

Library of Congress Cataloging in Publication Data

Denning, Michael.
   Cover Stories.
   (Popular fiction series)
   Bibliography: p.
   Includes index.
   1. Spy stories, English—History and criticism.
2. English fiction—20th century—History and criticism.
3. Politics in literature.   4. Great Britain in
literature.   5. Narration (Rhetoric)   I. Title.
II. Series.
PR888.S65D46   1987   823'.0872'09   86-21968

British Library CIP Data also available
ISBN 0-7100-9642-9

for Hazel

Series editors' preface

There are many good reasons for studying popular fiction. The best, though, is that it matters. In the many and varied forms in which they are produced and circulated – by the cinema, broadcasting institutions and the publishing industry – popular fictions saturate the rhythms of everyday life. In doing so, they help to define our sense of our selves, shaping our desires, fantasies, imagined pasts and projected futures. An understanding of such fictions – of how they are produced and circulated, organized and received – is thus central to an understanding of our selves; of how these selves have been shaped and of how they might be changed.

This series is intended to contribute to such an understanding by providing a context in which different traditions and directions in the study of popular fiction might be brought into contact so as to interanimate one another. It will thus range across the institutions of cinema, broadcasting and publishing, seeking to illuminate both their respective specificities as well as the relations between them with a view to identifying the ways in which popular film, television and writing interact as parts of developed cultural technologies for the formation of subjectivities. Consideration of the generic properties of popular fiction will thus be situated within an analysis of their historical and institutional conditions of production and reception.

Similarly, the series will represent, and coordinate a debate between, the diverse political perspectives through which the study of popular fiction has been shaped and defined in recent years. Feminist studies of the part popular fictions play in the production of gendered subjectivities and relations; Marxist perspectives on the relations between popular fictions and class formations; popular fiction as a site for the reproduction and contestation of subordinate racial and national identities: in encompassing contributions from these often sharply contrasting traditions of thought the series will explore the complex and intertwining web of political relations in which the production and reception of popular fictions are involved.

It should be clear, though, that in all this our aim is not to transform popular fiction into something else – into literature, say, or art cinema. If the study of popular fiction matters it is because what is ultimately at stake in such analysis is the production of a better popular fiction as well as of better, politically more productive ways of reading it.

Tony Bennett
Graham Martin

Contents

Acknowledgments

I began this book while studying at the Centre for Contemporary Cultural Studies, University of Birmingham, and my first debt is to the members of the Centre, particularly the English Studies Group. They offered advice, criticisms, and an approach to cultural studies that is, I hope, reflected in this book: though I have been away from Birmingham for a number of years, I continue to think of this as a 'Centre book.' At the risk of missing someone, let me thank in particular Dave Batchelor, Janet Batsleer, Tony Davies, Michael Green, Stuart Hall, Richard Johnson, Rebecca O'Rourke, Michael O'Shaughnessy, Bill Schwarz, and Roger Shannon.

Lars Engle, Carl Freedman, Fredric Jameson, J. Hillis Miller, and the members of the New Haven Marxist Literary Group all read and commented on early versions of Chapter 5; I also want to thank Jean-Christophe Agnew, Bob Horton, and Paul Joseph for sharing an enthusiasm for thrillers and their ideas about them. The series editors, Tony Bennett, Janet Woollacott, and Graham Martin, gave close and careful readings, offering criticisms and suggestions, and Philippa Brewster of Routledge & Kegan Paul encouraged the project at a very early stage and saw it through to the end.

Hazel Carby lived with these spies from the beginning at the Centre; I dedicate it to her as a small token of thanks.

Introduction

Let me lend you the History of Contemporary Society. It's in hundreds of volumes, but most of them are sold in cheap editions: *Death in Piccadilly, The Ambassador's Diamonds, The Theft of the Naval Papers, Diplomacy, Seven Days' Leave, The Four Just Men* . . .
— Arthur Rowe in Graham Greene, *The Ministry of Fear* (1943)

It is a habit in all of us to make our cover stories, our assumed personae, at least parallel with the reality . . . We should take the opposition's cover stories more seriously . . . The more identities a man has, the more they express the person they conceal . . . Few men can resist expressing their appetites when they are making a fantasy about themselves.
— George Smiley in John le Carré, *Tinker, Tailor, Soldier, Spy* (1974)

Since the turn of the century, spy thrillers have been 'cover stories' for our culture, collective fantasies in the imagination of the English-speaking world, paralleling reality, expressing what they wish to conceal, and telling the 'History of Contemporary Society.' Thrillers use cover stories about assumed identities and double agents, and take their plots from the cover stories of the daily news; and their tales of spies, moles, and the secret service have become a cover story, translating the political and cultural transformations of the twentieth century into the intrigues of a shadow world of secret agents. In the pages that follow I will look closely at some of these cover stories, at how they were put together, what forms they take, what history they tell and what they fail to tell, and what ideologies they narrate.

The spy thriller is ostensibly one of the most 'political' of popular fiction genres. Its subject is global politics: the Empire, fascism, communism, the Cold War, terrorism. Yet its political subject is only a pretext to the adventure formulas and the plots of betrayal, disguise, and doubles which are at the heart of the genre and of the reader's investment. So it is important to move beyond the manifest politics of these cover stories to their characteristic narrative structures in order to re-emerge with a sense of the ideologies of the forms themselves. This book will explore the ways the spy thriller narrates the crises and contradictions in ideologies of nation and Empire and of class and gender, seeing whether they subvert or reinforce the surface coding of the global politics of spies and counterspies. In doing this I will explore the relation between narrative structures and ideology, drawing on several bodies of theoretical work: marxist theories of ideology, the structuralist accounts of myth and narrative, and the continuing debates about realism. For what narratives are not cover stories? And what is ideology if not a cover story so deeply lived as to be almost unconscious, that necessary cover story by which the individual steps into daily life and its collective webs of work, language, and sexuality?

However, before proceeding, certain general questions about the analysis of popular fiction need be raised and at least tentatively considered. For why write (or read) *about* popular fiction at all? Common sense tells us that these cheap paperbacks and magazine serials are, as Graham Greene himself called them, 'entertainments,' meant for escape and relaxation, read on trains and buses, in odd moments between work, on holiday. Literary critics may find substance to analyze and interpret in 'literature,' but surely nothing more is needed for thrillers than a reviewer, alerting the reader to what is new and enjoyable (or perhaps old and revivable), or light reminiscences of authors and heroes, the 'inside story' for a particularly avid fan.

Against this common sense I see three justifications for writing and reading about popular fiction. The first might be seen as the interest of the sociologist or historian. These books have a place in a particular society, a particular history, a particular culture, and, like newspapers, diaries, or government documents, they can be used as evidence in reconstructing the lineaments of that history or culture. To a certain degree I will be doing this, and part of the concern of this book will be to see what these stories can tell us about twentieth-century British culture. But the historical reconstruction of twentieth-century British culture is not really my aim: if it were, the peculiar evidence supplied by spy thrillers would have to be put alongside a variety of other sorts of evidence. Furthermore, part of my argument will attempt to show what a tricky sort of historical evidence popular stories are, as I analyze the ruses of narrative representation.

This leads to a second justification for studying popular fiction which is closer to the interests of the literary critic. For 'literature,' that selected tradition of imaginative writing, is not separated absolutely or even self-evidently from the mass of imaginative writings that are produced in a society. Thus any study of 'literature' requires an analysis of how that category was itself established in a certain period as well as an account of the kinds of literary production against which it has been defined and which it excludes. Though the boundary between folk and oral narratives and literate narratives may be fairly well defined in non-capitalist societies, within capitalist societies the development of mass literacy and the subjection of almost all literary production to the market makes those boundaries between 'high' and 'low,' 'elite' and 'popular,' 'avant-garde' and 'mass,' extremely problematic. Indeed, though this book focuses primarily on popular fiction, it seems to me that the study of 'popular' fiction and the study of 'literary' fiction must not be seen as two separate disciplines but rather as parts of a reconstituted literary studies, that aspect of cultural studies which focuses on the production and consumption of narratives and figurative language.

The third justification for reading and writing about popular fiction is that these books are 'popular,' that is, that many people read them. This most obvious of justifications is also, I think, the trickiest. For I am not persuaded by the simple populist formula that they are the people's choice, that sales figures alone make these stories worthy of attention. First of all, this attitude tends to empty out all sense of criticism or interpretation and often leaves us with pure description: these are the stories that are popular. Second, it tends to empty out all sense of history: the books that used to be popular but are so no longer are forgotten or become the object of nostalgia. It seems to me that the point of writing or reading about popular fiction is not to ratify its popularity, nor to celebrate its universality, but rather to question the books that we do read for escape and relaxation, to stop and think about something 'natural,' something so much a part of our second nature, a part of everyday life, that we are not really sure of what it means or where it came from. The older books, now forgotten and hard to find, claim our attention not as nostalgia but as the history of our present reading, as the source of our own cherished stories, or even as the repressed alternatives to our own cover stories.

This then is my justification for other aspects of this project as well. For not only am I taking light entertainment very seriously, but I will, in what might be seen as undue magnification, train on it an array of lenses drawn from contemporary cultural theory. I will be looking as much at what is absent from these cover stories as at what is present, as much at the unintended possibilities the texts allow as at the authors' intentions. And I will argue that the significance of these stories lies as much in their form as in their content. Behind all of this is the intention to explore the two relations which Raymond Williams has usefully termed 'literature *in* society' and 'literature *and* society'; that is, first, looking at these thrillers as a form of cultural production within twentieth-century British society, and, second, looking at them as symptoms, representations, or productions of themes and currents within twentieth-century British culture.

To look at popular fiction in this way, to read and write *about* it, to search out the history of our relaxation, to look at our escapes through the complex lenses of narrative theory, to uncover the ideologies of the obvious, runs the risk of being as ridiculous as a record played at the wrong speed. I hope it can also, like a film in slow motion, show us motions not seen by the naked eye. In a wider way, I would hope that this study can contribute to the understanding of our present popular culture – its contradictory energies, its mystifications, and its utopian promises – in order to contribute to the ongoing and collective transformation to a socialist culture.

In what follows I will look first at three principal questions in the analysis of popular fiction: first, the question of genre, or simply, what is a thriller?; second, the question of literary history, or how does one tell the history of the thriller?; and third, the question of realism, or, what is the relation between thrillers and realist narrative and what does that mean for the much-vexed position of realism in socialist cultural debates? Then I will turn to four moments in the history of the thriller and look more closely at the texts and their situations.

Chapter 2 begins with the thrillers of the first two decades of the twentieth century, particularly those of John Buchan, E. Phillips Oppenheim, Erskine Childers, and 'Sapper' (H.C. McNeile), and will look at their relation to the crisis in Britain's world hegemony, and the compensatory ideologies of amateurism, popular imperialism and nationalism. In the third chapter I will look at the 'realist' anti-fascist thrillers of the young Eric Ambler in the 1930s and at their attempts to figure class and revolution as well as nation through stories of innocence lost. In the fourth chapter I will look at the James Bond stories of Ian Fleming and their highly successful fusion of traditional themes of Empire and England with the images and spectacles of the consumer society, particularly those around tourism and sexuality, in the late 1950s and early 1960s. And in Chapter 5 I turn to the spy novels of John le Carré and Graham Greene in the 1960s and 1970s and to the way their looking-glass wars and the figure of the 'mole,' personified by Kim Philby, narrate adventures of bureaucratic work in the secret states of 'post-industrial' capitalism. The conclusion will look at the documentary thrillers of Frederick Forsyth and Ken Follett of the 1970s and 1980s, with their elaborate secret histories, and then consider the political meanings and possibilities of the spy thriller at the present time.

There is one further issue to mention at the outset: as an American reader of these British spy thrillers, my relation to these cover stories is somewhat oblique; the references to them as 'our' entertainments obscures an important division in their audience between readers with a direct connection to the national and imperial ideologies of Great Britain and readers of English-language fiction generally. As I point out later, the fiction industry in contemporary Britain is heavily influenced by the sheer market consideration that the majority of its readers lie outside the boundaries of Britain. And though certain cover stories that the thriller narrates are not national and speak to audiences in a variety of English-speaking, industrial capitalist societies, other cover stories are explicitly 'English' and are read differently in different national contexts.

Nevertheless when I write of the audiences and the historical contexts of the spy thriller, I refer, with a few exceptions, to the British audience and to British social and cultural history. For despite my interest in issues of cultural reception, the moment and circumstances of production remain, to my mind, primary; though Fleming, le Carré, Follett, and others have found large American audiences, they have found few American competitors. The spy thriller has been, for most of its history, a British genre, indeed a major cultural export.

1
Thrillers, shockers, spy novels

Tinker, Tailor, Soldier, Spy: typologies of the spy thriller

> Thriller, One who or that which thrills; spec. (slang or colloq.) a sensational play or story (cf. shocker) 1896 *Pall Mall Mag* 'Full blown detectives . . . the sort you read of in the thrillers!'
>
> — *Oxford English Dictionary*

What is a spy thriller? Eric Ambler playfully writes that 'a spy story is a story in which the central character is a secret intelligence agent of one sort or another' and concludes that by this very reasonable definition he has never written one.[1] And for most of modern criticism this would be a small proof of Ambler's worth, a sign that he has disobeyed the genre, broken the rules, and written not spy novels but novels, perhaps even Literature (though at this writing Ambler, unlike Graham Greene, has not been so canonized). As the narrator of Ambler's *Cause for Alarm* says: 'Besides, who said that it was a spy story? It isn't.'

One can sympathize. Too often work on genre attempts to answer the question 'what is a spy thriller?' degenerates into mere classification and the construction of static typologies. One critic, interested in precisely distinguishing the spy novel from the detective story, the police procedural, the *roman noir*, science fiction, and the exotic adventure story, usefully demonstrates the false problems and inaccurate classifications made by previous writers. Unfortunately, by mixing the construction of an ideal type and the refining of this type by empirical testing, he is left with a definition no different from and no more useful than Ambler's off-the-cuff one: 'a dramatic novel where the protagonist works secretly in the service of a state.'[2] We are left with a definition so abstract as to tell us almost nothing and yet so narrow as to exclude Ambler's own work — work usually taken as one of the epitomes of the genre.

Nevertheless we do need a notion of genre before looking at a set of popular books which are produced as 'genre fiction'; so perhaps we can recast the question. Instead of asking 'what is a spy thriller?' or 'what are the elements necessary to make up a spy thriller?' we could ask: 'what does the reader expect when picking up a spy thriller?'; 'what forms, formulas, and conventions appear in spy thrillers?'; 'what meanings and ideologies are peculiar to these forms?' For a history of genres and formulas, far from being a sterile typological exercise, can become a crucial mediator between the individual narrative and social history, between text and society. Indeed, Fredric Jameson has argued that there is a privileged relation between genre theory and historical materialism:

> The strategic value of generic concepts for Marxism clearly lies in the mediatory function of the notion of a genre, which allows the coordination of immanent formal analysis of the individual text with the twin diachronic perspective of the history of forms and the evolution of social life . . . So generic affiliations, and the systematic deviation from them, provide clues which lead us back to the concrete historical situation of the individual text itself, and allow us to read its structure as ideology, as a socially symbolic act, as a protopolitical response to a historical dilemma.[3]

It is for this reason, to establish a mediator between the texts of John Buchan, Eric Ambler, Ian Fleming, and John le

Carré and the history of the British social formation, that I will begin by trying to outline the genre of the spy thriller and its formulas.

There are two main ways into the question of a popular genre, and I will call them, to begin with, the commercial definition and the formulaic definition. The first is the genre as it is defined in the marketplace as a particular sort of product; the second is its definition as a set of characteristic themes, stock characters, and conventional story patterns. The first, the commerical way into genre, is clearly very important to narratives that are produced primarily as commodities. These books are, in John Sutherland's phrase, 'categorized product,' and can be distinguished not only from other popular fiction genres but also from those popular novels which, though often formulaic, are not really genre fiction, those novels that we tend to call 'best-sellers.'

So someone looking for a spy thriller in W.H. Smiths will first find a rack of 'thrillers' which range across spy stories, masculine action tales, police procedurals, classic detective stories, and hardboiled private eye narratives. In the US these will be lumped under a general 'crime fiction' or 'mystery' rubric. Within this category, the genre of the 'spy thriller' appears not as a separate rack but as a few talismanic names endorsing the product, a canon of greats constructed by novelists, reviewers, and blurb writers. The offhand pontifical judgments quoted in book advertisements that Q.D. Leavis deplored in 1932 have developed into a fine art, and a cursory survey of spy thriller blurbs at a bookstore rack can give one more exact lineaments of the genre than many scholarly articles.

First, there is the unquestionable canon:

Of Eric Ambler: 'Unquestionably our best thriller writer' – Graham Greene

Of Graham Greene: 'The inventor of the modern spy'. – *Saturday Review*

Of Greene's *The Human Factor*: 'Probably the best espionage novel ever written' – UPI

Of Ian Fleming: 'The most forceful and driving writer of thrillers in England' – Raymond Chandler

Of John le Carré: 'The premier spy novelist of his time, perhaps of all time' – *Time*

Of le Carré's *The Spy Who Came in from the Cold*: 'The best spy story I have ever read' – Graham Greene

Then, the reprints of the early masters:

Of Erskine Childers: '*The Riddle of the Sands* is regarded by many as one of the best spy novels ever written; certainly it was the first modern espionage story and remains a classic of the genre . . . it is a novel that will appeal to scores of readers brought up on the realism of Eric Ambler, Graham Greene, and John le Carré.' – the Penguin blurb

Of John Buchan: *The Thirty-Nine Steps* set 'a pattern for adventure writers ever since' – Graham Greene

Of W. Somerset Maugham's *Ashenden*: '*Ashenden* is one of the two or three greatest spy stories ever written' – the Avon blurb

And, finally, the rank and file:

Of Francis Clifford: 'Not since Graham Greene was creating his adventures has there been a writer with such haunting quality.'

Of Len Deighton: 'The Raymond Chandler of the cloak and dagger set'; 'James Bond's most serious rival'; 'Without question the best since the days when Eric Ambler and Graham Greene were at the top of their form.'

Of Helen MacInnes: 'The queen of spy writers'; 'She can hang her cloak and dagger right there with Eric Ambler and Graham Greene.'

Of Geoffrey Household: 'In a class with Ambler, le Carré and Deighton.'

Of Gavin Lyall: 'Belongs to that too small shelf which contains the works of Eric Ambler and Geoffrey Household.'

Of Charles McCarry: 'In the tradition of the best espionage fiction, John Buchan to John le Carré'; 'A new and very welcome talent' – Eric Ambler

Of Ken Follett: 'A Winner . . . Ranks with le Carré, Ludlum, Graham Greene and Eric Ambler.'

Of Robert McCrum: 'Admirers of John le Carré should enjoy Robert McCrum.'

Though the reader may well be skeptical of this unending string of superlatives (and many more could have been added), advertising does have its rationality and the effect of these blurbs is to classify new books, to institutionalize veteran authors, and to create a certain horizon of expectation for reader and writer alike – in other words, to establish a genre. These blurbs are taken from the various apparatuses which surround the thriller: book reviews, anthologies, handbooks, essays by aficionados. And from these sources one can put together a brief history of the genre, a history that readers unconsciously absorb. Almost all commentators see the spy thriller as a predominantly British genre which finds its roots at the turn of the century: Erskine Childers's *The Riddle of the Sands* (1903) is often taken as the first spy novel. From there the spy thriller is incarnated in the adventures of John Buchan's Richard Hannay (particularly *The Thirty-Nine Steps*, 1915) and Sapper's Bull-dog Drummond (1920s), in the 'realism' of Somerset Maugham's *Ashenden* (1928) and the early novels of Eric Ambler and Graham Greene (1930s), in the explosion of Ian Fleming's James Bond in the 1950s, in the cynical and polished tales of John le Carré and Len Deighton (1960s), and in the massively documented 'secret histories' of Frederick Forsyth and Ken Follett (1970s).

The problem with this sort of genre definition is that it conflates the impulse toward a star system in the mass market with the notion of a 'great tradition' in traditional literary criticism, producing a sort of paraliterary canon, an ideal order of master *auteurs*, devoid of any historical understanding. Indeed, all too many critics of the thriller have accepted this essentially commercial definition of genre because of its compatibility with literary-critical practice. Though I will be looking at the work of some of the leading *auteurs* of the thriller, the importance of genre study should be to situate their texts within the set of institutions — formula, style, reading public, publishing — which constitute a genre rather than to ratify a particular canon.

The second main way into genre is by defining its characteristic formulas and then constructing certain typologies.[4] In most thriller criticism, this has led to two sorts of defining oppositions within the genre. First, there has been the almost universal distinction between 'realistic' and 'fantastic,' between the realism of Ambler and le Carré and the romance of Fleming.[5] I will examine this pervasive commonsense opposition in the section on realism. The second opposition is made between types of protagonists, sometimes between amateurs and professionals, at other times between heroic adventurers and cynical or confused muddlers. With a simple combination, one can find heroic amateurs (Buchan's Richard Hannay), heroic professionals (Fleming's James Bond), confused amateurs (Ambler's Charles Latimer or Josef Vadassy), and confused professionals (le Carré's George Smiley).[6] Similarly this sort of taxonomy can establish differences between spy thrillers (where the protagonist may or may not be a professional spy) and other genres — private eyes, detectives, policemen.

In more complex versions, certain conventional story patterns are isolated and classified. Tzvetan Todorov, in his essay 'Typologies of Detective Fiction,' makes a logical rather than an empirical or historical distinction between mystery plots and thriller plots.[7] The mystery, he argues, consists of two superimposed stories: the story of a crime and the story of an investigation. In the purest form of the mystery, the classical detective story, the first story is the significant one but is absent. The second story, the present one, is the relatively transparent tale of how the first story came to be known. Moving across a spectrum to the thriller, there is a shift in emphasis from the first story to the second, and the crime becomes a mere pretext to a series of adventures and can eventually be replaced by a mission (a search or a quest). Todorov maintains that the two ends of this spectrum work on two different sorts of interest: the mystery, on curiosity which proceeds from effect to cause (from the corpse to revelation of murderer); the thriller, on suspense which moves from cause to effect (from villain with gun to daring escape). So what is interesting is not the absolute differences between commercially established genres – detectives, spies, private eyes, etc. – but the syntax of plot, the way the permutations of mission, hunt, and investigation are worked, the way the hunter/hunted dialectic is articulated in varieties of what we might call masculine romance.[8] This is a plot to which we will return, heeding Julian Symons's observation that 'almost all of the best thrillers are concerned, in one form or another, with the theme of the hunted man.'[9]

Another way of defining the genre's formula is not by type of hero nor by conventional story pattern but by characteristic theme, the particular vision of the world the genre projects. There are two main ways the spy thriller can be so categorized. First, the world of the thriller is one of international politics and intrigue, of multinational economic organizations. It is no accident that the genre first appears at the beginning of the twentieth century, in the imperialist stage of capitalism when the existence of rival imperialist states and a capitalist world system made it increasingly difficult to envision the totality of social relations as embodied in any single 'knowable community.' The novel of espionage is the tale of the boundary between nations and cultures, and the spy acts as a defender or subverter of the nation in the face of the other, the alien. The spy story appears in Britain in the wake of the heroic novels of imperial adventure and narrates the threat to the Empire. The spy became the figure for the fortunes of Empire in Britain, providing explanations for its decline and betrayal.

Indeed, one can see the spy novel in the terms that Georg Lukács, the marxist theorist and historian of the novel, used in his account of the modernist novel. Faced, in a period of imperialism and monopoly, with the inability to narrate the totality of social relations in the terms of individual experience, a number of short cuts were invented which magically reconciled individual experience with an increasingly reified and incomprehensible social order. Among these solutions Lukács identified the symbolists' inflation of the meaningless everyday detail to epiphanic transcendence, and the naturalists' aspiration to a complete positivist description and inventory of the social world. The solution invented by the spy novel was less complex and more ingenious: it kept a fairly traditional plot by making the spy the link between the actions of an individual – often an 'ordinary person' – and the world historical fate of nations and empires. History is displaced to secret conspiracies and secret agents, from politics to ethics. The secret *agent* returns human *agency* to a world which seems less and less the product of human action.

The other side of this 'solution' is that the spy thriller transforms an incomprehensible political situation (or a situation the knowledge of which is being repressed) into the ethical categories of masculine romance, the battle of hero and villain becoming one between Good and Evil, the forces of light and the forces of darkness. A number of writers on the thriller have noted this and I will attempt later to untangle the political codings of this ethical binary: are the political aspects of these books simply fillers for the more significant ethical opposition, or does this Good/Evil opposition have a political and ideological significance of its own?

These are some preliminary speculations on the thriller as genre; the difficulty with them is that they remain tied to a literary criticism which has eternal modes – romance, tragedy, melodrama, and so forth – into which new variations can be slotted without much consideration of the historical situation they respond to or the ideological functions they serve. At its worst this can lead to finding spy stories in Homer or seeing James Bond as a modern Lancelot.

So I would like to recast these two modes of genre study and foreground their kernels of history. Thus if the commercial definition of genre can lead to a star system crossed with the great tradition, it can also provide the beginning of a way of looking at what Terry Eagleton has called the 'literary mode of production.' And the various interesting typologies of heroes, plots and themes that critics have constructed can be put into motion by reinserting them into a particular historical situation. Indeed, we can add to John Cawelti's somewhat neutral term, 'formula,' Fredric Jameson's notion of an 'ideologeme.'[10] The term, an attempt to fuse narrative analysis with ideological critique, is less a solution than a reminder that themes and formulas in popular fiction never appear inertly, simply to be catalogued, but emerge as part of antagonistic collective discourses. Thus my aim in the following pages is to try to account for the social history of the thriller in terms of its relations of production and consumption, and in terms of the ideologemes articulated in its characteristic formulas.

Yesterday's spy: toward a history of the thriller

If genre remains an uncertain if necessary concept in the cultural study of popular fiction, history, which rescued us from static canonic and taxonomic notions of genre, is no less uncertain. Recent developments in literary theory have for the most part focused on ways of reading, on the intricacies of decoding literary messages, and have not fully addressed ways of thinking about the history of various types of literary production. An established mainstream literary historian who once wrote that literary history was the record of transcendent works now finds 'transcendence' a somewhat unclear historiographic concept but has little to put in its place.[11] And a leading marxist critic, in a book that revises the history of the novel, insists that 'although literary history is here everywhere implied,' his book should not 'be taken as a paradigmatic work in this discursive form or genre, which is today in crisis.'[12] The history of popular fiction is in no less disarray.

For the most part, the history of popular fiction is told as the history of 'great' authors; as Michael Gilbert writes, in 'tracing the history of the spy story, we move from peak to peak.' And there are a number of these brief histories of the spy thriller which focus on the sequence of the major *auteurs* of the genre.[13] But this sort of history, though useful, is inadequate. As I have already argued, this impulse to create a canon of great writers, an impulse drawn from traditional literary history, has a curious resemblance to the star system of the market, and what looks like history becomes simply the construction of a timeless pantheon of all-time bestsellers.

Indeed, rather than replicating the dilemmas of traditional literary history, the history of popular fiction could reorient literary studies in the way that recent social history has reoriented historical studies generally. For in historical studies, the dissatisfaction with a predominantly narrative political history focusing on the actions of highly visible individuals gave rise to a social history whose concern was with the behavior and culture of groups and classes of people, with their patterns of work and everyday life, and with their symbolic languages. So in popular fiction history, we should turn away from the central focus on the intentions and actions of individual authors and toward an analysis of groups and classes of fiction, of narrative patterns and figurative language, of the production and consumption of these narratives, and of the culture of which they form a part.

But to say this is not to solve the problem. For immediately, in the study of popular fiction, two possible routes open up, and it is difficult to take both. On the one hand, one might write a history of the books – how they were published, who read them, what functions they served, how many copies were sold, what the conditions of authorship were – the questions usually lumped under the rubric 'sociology of literature.'[14] On the other hand, one might write the history of important narrative patterns and figures – why different genres rise and fade, the structure and meaning of particular plots or metaphors, the relation of these narratives and figures to other aspects of society. The most substantive analyses of spy thrillers have taken this route, but they tend to be quite weak historically, usually falling back on some version of archetypal or myth-and-symbol criticism.[15]

Very rarely do these two histories meet. The first type is usually written by historians and sociologists who are only marginally concerned with the content of the books they count or the interpretations of those stories made by the readers they investigate. For the most part they accept the notion that popular fiction is a form of escape and relaxation, and that serious analysis of the stories themselves is beside the point, the point being a history of publishing or a history of leisure and recreation.

The second type of history is usually written by renegade literary critics, and though it has produced persuasive interpretations of popular fiction, it all too often reduces the historical project to a loosely sketched 'context' and rarely pays much attention to the details of publishing or the reading public. There have been important exceptions to this separation of the two projects, most notably in Q.D. Leavis's classic *Fiction and the Reading Public*, in the work of Louis James on nineteenth-century popular fiction and of John Sutherland on twentieth-century bestsellers, and in the work of the Birmingham Centre's English Studies group.[16]

Nevertheless, at this point, an adequate integration of these different histories into a single popular fiction history seems unlikely. Changes in popular fiction genres, narrative formulas, and characteristic figures are overdetermined: by forces within the form, the formal efforts at verisimilitude, parody, and stylization; by forces within the fiction industry, by changes in publishing, in the reading public, and in the conception of the 'literary'; and by forces in the culture at large, by changes in patterns of work and leisure, in versions of masculinity and femininity, in the construction of nation and empire, and in the conflict of classes. What I will attempt to do is to juxtapose some of these histories – to outline some shifts in the publishing of the thriller, in its reading public, and, in the following section, in its dominant formulas.

The word 'thriller' came into use in the 1880s and 1890s together with 'shocker' as a designation for the proliferating cheap sensational fiction which emerged at the moment when a mass-produced culture started to come into being in Britain, a moment signaled by the Education Act of 1870 and by the creation of *Pearson's Weekly* (1890), Newnes's *Tit-bits* (1881), and Harmsworth's *Daily Mail* (1896), the first popular daily newspaper. By the first decades of the twentieth century, the imperial adventure tales of H. Rider Haggard, Arthur Conan Doyle, and Robert Louis Stevenson, which were often aimed at schoolboys, were being supplanted by the first thrillers, the stories of William Le Queux (beginning in 1891), E. Phillips Oppenheim (beginning in 1887), and the king of them all, Edgar Wallace (beginning in 1905), which were aimed at an adult male audience.

The emergence of this new popular genre was in part due to shifts in the publishing industry, and I can outline these briefly by drawing on the excellent recent work of John Sutherland.[17] The new 'thrillers' or 'shockers' were read in three main forms: as single-volume hardcover novels rented from the circulating libraries, as short stories in the magazines and story papers, and as serials in the popular press. The first two of these forms were spurred by a major change in fiction publishing in the late 1890s: the demise of the three-decker novel, the three-volume, 31s. 6d. form which had been standard throughout most of the nineteenth century for all novels. This form had been supported by the commercial subscription libraries, led by Mudie's Circulating Library. The libraries were the main buyers of three-decker novels, and hence dominated the production of fiction.

The return of the single-volume novel coincided with the establishment of cheaper circulating libraries by W.H. Smiths and Boots. The 6s. or 7s. 6d. novel hired at the station Smiths, the High Street Boots, or the local news-agent's twopenny library, dominated fiction production and consumption from 1894 to 1944. Throughout this period English readers were more a book-borrowing than a book-buying public, and when Q.D. Leavis surveyed the book market in 1932, she found that the circulating libraries were patronized primarily by the lower-middle class, by school teachers and clerical workers, particularly by women who would change books for themselves and their families several times a week, choosing a high proportion of fiction over non-fiction. The circulating libraries became a major force in mass production of fiction; and they found it most profitable to buy large numbers of a few books, and to rely on established authors. Edgar Wallace, the most successful thriller writer of the period (though he wrote few spy stories, since espionage was not yet the dominant theme in thrillers), was, as Graham Greene wrote, one of 'a phenomenon which might have been invented by Balzac – the human book factory,' writing 150 novels in twenty-seven years. Indeed, the figure that might best characterize this period would be a Hodder & Stoughton Yellow Jacket edition of an Edgar Wallace thriller. The H & S Yellow Jackets, 'the ubiquitous hardback library that became far and away the most familiar series of all to the between-the-wars thriller fan,' included books by Le Queux, Oppenheim, Buchan, and Sapper as well as Wallace, and they were bought in such quantity by the W.H. Smith rental libraries that a rival publisher described the Smiths bookstalls as Hodder & Stoughton depots.[18]

The breakup of the three-decker monopoly also led to a revival of fiction in the magazines, which ranged from the established middle-class monthlies like the *Strand*, to the popular story monthlies and weeklies that appeared in the wake of *Pearson's* and *Tit-bits*, to the boys' weeklies. The *Strand* published the best-known and highest-paid writers from Conan Doyle (the Sherlock Holmes stories), to Oppenheim and Wallace. But the principal outlets for thrillers were the magazines like *The Thriller, Detective Weekly*, and *World Stories of Thrills and Adventure*, published for a working-class and lower-middle-class audience by the Amalgamated Press, the Newnes Group, and Thomson & Leng. Thrillers also gradually began to displace school stories as the main attraction of boys' weeklies, particularly after the influx of the American pulp magazines, the 'Yank mags.'

The next major shift in the production and consumption of popular fiction came with the Second World War; Sutherland dates it at 1944. And if the first period might be called the age of Edgar Wallace, this period beginning in 1944 is, as Sutherland aptly points out, the age of Graham Greene. The three main aspects of the new organization of popular fiction are the public library, the book club, and the paperback. The expansion of the public library system by the postwar Labour government, the move by public libraries into stocking popular fiction, and the decline of the circulating libraries made the public library the largest patron of crime fiction. Sutherland has argued that the public library dominance of fiction has had a number of consequences for the novel: on the one hand, unlike Boots and Smiths, which bought many copies of the most popular novels, the public libraries tend to buy fewer copies of more novels, thus supporting lesser-known authors; on the other hand, the library's patronage has warped British literary production toward novels which are short, frequent (one a year from an author), and acceptable to a wide audience sharing the middle-class 'culture of the ratepayer.' I will look later at the effects of these constraints on the thriller, but it is clear that the reading of the novels of Ambler, Greene, and le Carré is as tied to the public library as was that of Wallace to the circulating libraries.

Perhaps the most direct descendant of the circulating libraries has been the book club, which was first developed in the 1920s and 1930s. However, the book clubs have been principally reprint houses, since until 1968 they were prohibited from simultaneous publishing. Nevertheless they have effects: unlike libraries, they focus on large sales of a small number of books, but like libraries they cater to a suburban middle-class culture. They have often pushed writers of 'genre fiction' toward that amorphous center of middlebrow popular fiction, the 'bestseller,' which is the main stock of the book club. The entanglement of the spy thriller of the Ambler, Greene and le Carré vintage with the book club might be seen by the two ends of Greene's career as a thriller writer: *Stamboul Train*, his first 'entertainment,' 'saved' his career as a novelist when it was chosen in 1931 as a selection by the Book Society, the pioneer British book club;[19] and in 1978 *The Human Factor*, his first full-fledged spy *novel* (no longer an 'entertainment'), was a choice of the Book Club Associates, the largest book club in Britain and owned by W.H. Smith.

The third wing of the post-World War II organization of popular fiction is the paperback book, and this has had somewhat different effects than either the public library or the book club. The paperback revolution in Britain occurred later than its American counterpart despite — indeed, because of — the unique enterprise of Penguin books. Unlike Penguins, which were 'respectable,' sold in bookstores, and carried a range of fiction and non-fiction, the American Pocket Books, begun in 1939 by Robert de Graaf, became the chief vehicle for popular fiction, particularly the hardboiled stories that had developed in the pulp magazines. Cheap, with lurid covers, sold in drugstores and railway stations, and given a great boost by the Armed Services Editions circulated during World War II, Pocket Books and its many imitators dominated American popular fiction. This breakthrough in the paperback thriller in Britain did not occur until the early 1960s with the emergence of Pan Books, and it was tied to the spy thriller: for in 1965, of Pan's 21 million paperback sales, 6 million were from Ian Fleming's James Bond novels, and, of the first eighteen million-selling paperbacks in Britain, ten were Bond books.[20] I will return to some of the consequences of this in the chapter on Fleming.

With this sketchy periodization of the means of production and distribution of popular fiction in mind, I will turn to the relations of consumption, the question of the reading public. This is a vexed question in literary theory today and it can be separated into two different but equally important questions: who read a particular body of fiction? and how was that fiction read? The first question has led to a small but substantial body of empirical work on the reading public. The second question, how fiction is read, has led to the growing body of reader-response criticism, 'reception-aesthetics.' This orthodox literary criticism of reading has remained thoroughly ahistorical and finds itself in a peculiar double bind: either a text has an implied reader within it determining the way it is read (and thus reception can be deduced from the text itself) or an almost infinite number of readings or misreadings are possible. The notion that there are class ways of reading – historically determined patterns of reading specific to a particular class, gender, or race sharing a particular culture – and that these ways of reading might be specified, has not been developed sufficiently, though there are important moves toward this in George Orwell's essays on popular fiction and the way it is read in working-class communities, in Richard Hoggart's *The Uses of Literacy*, and in the work of the Birmingham Centre's English Studies Group.

It is at this point that we can see some of the limits of studying a genre: for a focus on a particular popular fiction genre and its reading public produces a somewhat different knowledge than, for example, a focus on a particular reading public, that is, on a particular class culture or group culture and its reading matter (or its recreations and symbolic activities). Increasingly, the study of popular culture has turned from a text-centered or artifact-centered object of study to an attempt to outline the ways of life, the ways of struggle of the 'popular classes.'

By temporarily assuming the culture as object rather than the text as object we can begin to see the limits of a genre study, limits that ought be kept in mind throughout this work. First, a genre is not a self-contained body of texts; it is a part of a range of popular stories read in a variety of forms — in books, bought or borrowed, in newspapers or magazines; it is also part of a range of popular reading matter which includes the popular press, sporting papers, Sunday papers, cookbooks, technical manuals, and school texts; and it is only part of that culture's narrative entertainment which includes at different times music halls, radio, movies, and television. Some of the characteristic ideologemes we isolate in thrillers may be shared, or contradicted, by narrative patterns in other parts of the popular culture. So when historians of the working class or the lower-middle class write their chapters on 'leisure,' 'culture,' or 'recreations,' the reading of thrillers usually takes up no more than a paragraph. So the choice of a set of texts as an object of study results in an implicit foregrounding and magnification.

Second, a genre cannot be seen as a self-contained object, because it is, like any established set of conventions, historical. So just as we must look at the internal history of a genre, we must also consider the genre as itself a symptom and marker of historical change. The spy thriller emerges at a certain moment in the history of a particular society, is transformed, and will no doubt end at some point. Even during its lifetime it may at one time be a dominant genre in the field of popular fiction and at other times be a subordinate one, defined either by its novelty, its cult audience, its lack of commercial or aesthetic self-consciousness, or its residual nature. In order to see this, one must view a genre in a system of genres, establishing it by its differences.

Despite these limitations, there are some important angles of vision that the focus on a particular genre can give us. First, it can give us a narrative rather than simply a philosophical or institutional notion of ideology. When focusing on a class or group culture, the ideology of that class or group is usually defined as either a world view, a system of ideas and values that can be outlined as a philosophy, or as the 'false consciousness' which reproduces exploitative social relations through the institutions of social control – the schools, law, churches, etc. Characterizing ideology as essentially narrative can avoid the tendency of the first definition toward a simple history of ideas and the tendency of the second toward a functionalism by seeing that ideology, far from being a set of ideas that one chooses to believe or disbelieve or that are true or false, is composed of the stories individuals tell themselves in order to make the vast collective systems of work and sexuality comprehensible in individual terms. These stories permit the recognition of contradictions at the same time as they establish conventional ways of managing and resolving those contradictions. Thus a study of popular narratives has a purchase which the study of other recreations may not – for these narratives are not only *of* the culture but are *about* the culture.

The second angle of vision that the study of genre gives is the reminder that there are not 'pure' class cultures; for if the genre 'thriller' can become reified so too can the entity 'working-class culture.' The reading public of popular fiction crosses class; it may be the culture of the 'people' but it is not the culture of any particular class. Popular culture does not belong to one class or another; it is a field of cultural struggle whose boundaries are constantly shifting, and whose signs can be read in different ways by different audiences. This takes us back to the question of the reading public of 'thrillers,' for thrillers offer a peculiar way of combining the empirical question of who read these stories and the more speculative question of how people read them, how they were interpreted and made sense of. For there seems to be a distinct shift in the class composition of the reading public of spy thrillers. The early thriller of Wallace, Buchan, and Sapper was the basic reading stock of working-class and lower-middle-class men and boys, and, inversely, they made up a substantial, though not entire, body of the readership. Nicholas Blake wrote in 1942 that 'it is an established fact that the detective-novel proper is read almost exclusively by the upper and professional classes. The so-called "lower-middle" and "working" classes tend to read "bloods", thrillers.' And Q.D. Leavis, in her survey of the reading public, divides that public into 'highbrow,' 'middlebrow,' and 'lowbrow'; the 'lowbrow' audience is largely lower-middle-class and working-class and its reading material includes the thriller.[21]

The shift in generic patterns initiated by Ambler and Greene and completed by le Carré and Len Deighton, the complex shift from the 'blood' to the 'spy novel' with which I will be dealing, marks not only a formal shift toward greater 'realism' nor simply an ideological shift but also a shift in the class of the reading public as the spy thriller becomes increasingly the reading matter of professional and managerial men. The question of how this genre's working-class audience evolved into a middle-class one will concern us throughout the book; perhaps through this question we can begin to see how these different publics read these stories and what they made of them.

The great game of realism

> ... history does not prove games wrong, anymore than games prove history so ...
> — Len Deighton, *Spy Story* (1973)

Despite Len Deighton's accurate sense of the relative autonomy of games and history, his own games and histories — carefully documented spy thrillers, popular military histories, and counter-factual historical fictions of Nazi rule in Britain — play with the 'real' in such a way that the simple assertion that they do not disprove each other, the refusal of a naive 'realism,' is itself part of the game. So too any attempt to establish a relation between history and those peculiar games known as spy thrillers raises the much-debated issue of 'realism.' I will deal with realism and the thriller for two reasons: first, because almost all critics of the thriller have at some point reached for the label of 'realism' in the course of their explanations, and second, because much of the socialist and marxist debate about popular culture has focused on the ideological meaning and function of realism. It is worth emphasizing at the outset that 'realism' is a term with many meanings; however, the two logical strategies – either to define it ourselves for the sake of consistency or to dismiss it on the grounds that it can never be made to mean anything specific – are not adequate. Rather it is necessary to see that realism has different significances within different aesthetics. Thus it can signify a number of different formal devices (for example, representationalism, sociological description, an emphasis on the narrative of an individual, the use of 'common' language, etc.) and a number of divergent views of the real (for example, scientistic determinism, bourgeois individualism, anti-clerical secularism, positivism, historical materialism). To define any particular 'realism' is to define the aesthetic of which it forms part, and to juxtapose different meanings of realism can be a useful way of juxtaposing these different aesthetics.

The basic working opposition used by many critics and writers of the thriller is that between realism and romance, between 'realistic' spy stories and 'fantastic' thrillers. It is so common as to be part of the aesthetic ideology of the thriller, and it is used in two basic ways, as a synchronic mapping of the genre and as a diachronic construct that serves to explain the history of the genre. In the first case the opposition is cast as the legacy of the two literary precursors of the genre, the two figures whose novels about spies did not make them 'spy novelists,' but whose influence created the anxiety under which later thriller writers labored: Rudyard Kipling and Joseph Conrad. For the heroic romance of adventure, of spying in defense of the Empire, the story of the 'Great Game,' comes from Kipling's *Kim* (1900), and the cynical, realistic story of intrigue, betrayal and double agents was established by Conrad's *The Secret Agent* (1907) and *Under Western Eyes* (1911).

Along with this family romance of more heroic parents, the opposition between romance and realism is often used as an explanation of the history of the genre. Ambler himself writes that Buchan's spy stories 'achieved a higher level of reality than those of Oppenheim,' and that

Maugham's stories were yet another advance in realism. Anthony Boucher argues that Ambler's 'meticulously detailed realism' transfigured the spy story, and countless critics saw the novels of le Carré and Deighton as more 'real' than those of Fleming. One spy thriller aficionado, Donald McCormick, writes of the 'quest of ultra-realism' among thriller writers, constantly compares the fiction with the real world of espionage, and judges writers by their authenticity. Much is made of the 'fact' that the KGB and the CIA comb Len Deighton's novels for the details of each other's espionage work, and McCormick offers a list of the novelists who were actually engaged in intelligence work. Ambler's authenticity is more amazing, in McCormick's eyes, in that he was never in a secret service.[22]

Other critics are more skeptical. Despite the espionage experience of Ian Fleming and the footnotes and appendices of Len Deighton, Bruce Merry argues that spy thrillers are not mimetic: 'the narrative image rarely corresponds to the known and ascertainable facts about real life spy networks and intelligence operations.'[23] No doubt both McCormick and Merry have a kernel of truth. There is, probably, a measure of accuracy in the details of contemporary spy novels, though I will not attempt to prove or disprove it. Deighton and others probably do do some of the research McCormick so admires. And it is just as likely that the 'narrative images' – the usual plot structures, the adventures of the Smileys as well as of the Bonds – do not correspond to actual intelligence work.

But both critics miss the point: as Deighton himself says, 'history does not prove games wrong, anymore than games prove history so.' We must recast the debate about 'realism' in terms other than simple accuracy or inaccuracy. And here the classic formulation of realism by the marxist theorist of the novel, Georg Lukács, is provisionally very helpful. For Lukács shows that this debate about fidelity to detail, strict representationalism, is a false problem. Realism is not simple authenticity of detail and fidelity to the individual 'facts' of history; nor is it the application of a pre-established theory of history to the novel, the dressing up of concepts as characters, a vast allegory or fictionalized sociology. Realism, for Lukács, is based not on the distinction between reality and fiction, not on a notion of the world and its verbal mirror, but on the distinction between narration and description.

Surprisingly, perhaps, the narration—description distinction is common in structuralist analyses of narrative as well, though it is coded in linguistic terms. Thus Todorov makes the distinction between 'narrative verbs' and 'narrative adjectives,' A.J. Greimas between dynamic and static predicates. Other versions which are similar are the doing/being and the function/index of Roland Barthes, and Vladimir Propp's function/attribute. Though these are not exactly the same in every case, they are similar efforts to divide narrative into those aspects dealing with the processes involving the agents and those dealing with the state of the agents. What is distinctive about Lukács is his ideological translation of this opposition; he argues that the overdevelopment of description at the expense of narration leads to a loss in the ability of the novel to render its specific form of knowledge – a knowledge of the world in terms of change, process and time, a sense of the totality of social relations in terms of individual lived experience, and a knowledge of the world from the point of view of the participant rather than of the observer: 'narration establishes proportions, description merely levels'; 'description contemporizes everything, narration recounts the past.'

Of particular interest to us, then, is his critique of naturalism, of those novelists, figured in his work by Emile Zola, who foregrounded the close, detailed description of aspects of social life. This led to a 'disintegration of the composition into disconnected and autonomous details,' according to Lukács; 'the naturalists aspire to even greater technical "precision" in terminology; in increasing measure they employ the jargon of the field with which they are dealing.'[24] At this point we can see the nature of the spy thriller's 'ultra-realism' that McCormick celebrates, the trade jargon of Deighton and Trevanian, the painstaking descriptions of espionage tradecraft, the forest of acronyms.

And we can see why, despite this surface realism, the realism of the 'narrative image,' in Merry's phrase, is still in doubt. For all the painstaking research, the jargon, and the occasional historical characters are clever technical tricks, superlative effects of the real, covering, as Graham Greene said of Edgar Wallace, 'an almost incredible story with very precise realistic details.'[25] To call this 'realism' is not adequate.

But this is not an end; for the question arises as to the relation between these extremely effective reality-effects in the description of the thriller and the narration proper. For, unlike naturalism, in only a few cases does description dominate the narration to the point that we feel the plot doesn't really matter: one thinks of the early thrillers of Deighton where what one recalls is more the tone than the plot. For the most part, however, description is in the service of the narration.

Here one can turn to Lukács's other, complementary definition of realism – not just the proper foregrounding of the narration but also the figuring of the totality of social processes. Measured this way, the spy novel, despite its preservation of plot, has a strategic containment of realism in its short-cut to the totality; as I have argued earlier, its focus on the world of espionage does not necessarily make it about spies. Rather the intelligence community serves as a shadowy figure for the social world of late capitalism where the opacities that surround human agency are cut through by projecting an essentially magical figure, the secret agent. Thus, the spy novel, like those other sub-genres of the twentieth-century novel which create a sub-world cut off from any productive labor – the Hollywood novel, the university novel, etc. – is only a feigned realism, a sleight-of-hand totality.

Nevertheless, to point out that representationalism and a host of real facts about espionage do not realism make, and to further point out that the strategic containments of the genre itself would make it very unlikely that spy thrillers could be considered realist in the sense of the classic nineteeth-century realist novels, does not entirely solve our problem. We have yet to *explain* the perceived distinction between realistic and romantic thrillers, or to explain why a somewhat different socialist discourse about realism than that of Lukács would see these texts as realism. I will take the second point first.

Much socialist and marxist criticism has revolved around the concept of realism. One tradition, figured most prominently by Lukács, has maintained a privileged position for realism for its grasp of the totality of social relations, its construction of 'typical' characters and situations to render social processes through the experiences of participants rather than through the contemplative isolation of observers, and for its attention to the tenor of daily life. However, there is another tradition, advocates of avant-garde practices in the arts, who maintain that realism as a genre is no more than a historically limited set of devices that produce the effect of reality, and that this effect confirms the naturalness of narrative, its focus on individual agents, its varieties of closure, its placing of the reader or viewer in a position of unproblematic knowledge, and ultimately its reproduction of the common sense of everyday life. For these critics what was once a critical, demystifying genre, one which decoded earlier allegorical modes, has now become itself heavily coded, naturalizing the conventions of capitalist society, and confirming the habits of mind and the popular plots that make up everyday ideology. What is needed, these critics argue, is an artistic practice that transgresses accepted codes and disrupts the frames and ways of seeing that are part of our mental baggage.

Like the Lukácsian account and defense of realism, this marxist modernism has cast its claims largely in terms of literature, and has paid little attention to popular fiction. However, recently, given the fact that many aspects of the armature of the classic realist novel have survived and been highly codified in varieties of popular fiction – in the middlebrow novel, a descendant of the domestic novel, in the bestseller's debt to naturalism, and even in those more closed forms like the thriller and the mystery – the critique of realism and of representational and narrative modes has been extended to popular fiction.[26]

Now a certain amount of ahistorical formalism has impeded this discussion: surely Lukács is more useful as a historian analyzing the strategies and ideologies of both nineteenth-century realism and twentieth-century modernism than as a moralist maintaining that a particular historical form − nineteenth-century realism − will always embody the knowledge of social processes that marks 'realism' generally. And the modernists surely mistake Lukács's sense of realism if they reduce it to mere representationalism, particularly given his critique of that peculiar modernist representationalism known as naturalism. As Terry Eagleton has pointed out in a particularly useful consideration of realism and popular culture, it is a formalism to maintain that any particular form has a necessary ideological significance at all times. 'It would certainly be a mistake,' Eagleton argues, 'to say that popular culture is always culture which "naturalizes the sign", which is always therefore, in Barthes' sense, mythological, and that *that's* its ideological potency.'[27] Both literary and popular texts can be either highly code-governed or code-transgressive: neither of these has any necessary privilege.

However, the most difficult aspect of this debate for the thriller is that its terms − for both parties − are realism and modernism, whereas the discussion of the thriller is cast in terms of an older opposition, that between realism and romance. For though narration is as central to the thriller as to the realist novel, the narration is not based on the paradigms of the realist novel − the biography with its stages of education, self-consciousness, and disillusionment − but on the paradigms of the masculine adventure romance: the hunt, the contest, the game. The question then becomes: why does this older, non-novelistic, sometimes allegorical adventure mode survive and remain popular? And what does this mean for a marxist critical discourse which has often taken 'realism' as surpassed and old-fashioned?

First, we must not see this as a simple survival, as if a

pre-capitalist romance continued to flourish, and Bull-dog Drummond were merely a latter-day knight. On the contrary, as Martin Green has shown in his history of the adventure story, the modern adventure is a combination of elements from older romance with an individualism, representationalism, and a concern for capitalist technique that it shares with the novel: within the adventure tale, there is a tension between what he calls chivalric adventures and mercantile adventures. Furthermore, he shows that the survival of the adventure mode into capitalist culture is closely tied to imperialism.[28]

I would argue further that this hybrid form is nourished by a popular audience which has not yet been disciplined to read stories as novels, as tales of 'individuals': that popular allegory from religious traditions (like *The Pilgrim's Progress*) combines with the mutualistic solidarities of working-class culture to favor the development of modern allegorical forms like melodrama, adventures, and thrillers at the expense of bourgeois realism.

Finally, the centrality of the hunt, the contest, and the game – aspects of these stories which are originally drawn from the pursuits of the gentry – find a new relevance in a world where games and leisure are increasingly a separate sphere of working-class culture, as the rise in spectator sports would attest. Indeed, an attention to games can explain the nature of the 'formal' distinction between romantic and realistic thrillers. For the game is central to the thriller. 'The Great Game,' Kipling's term for the secret service in *Kim*, fitted the boy's fantasy of living between two cultures, English *and* Indian, a sort of double agent without the anxiety of the Cold War, but it also stuck as a term for espionage in succeeding thrillers. In the early thrillers, sporting abilities are not only a prerequisite for the hero but supply much of the pleasure of the text. In Childers's *The Riddle of the Sands*, one is deluged with detailed accounts of small-craft sailing; it is that knowledge, that expertise, that lends verisimilitude to the tale of two amateur sailors foiling the German plot to invade England. The serial contests of Bull-dog Drummond, the amateur boxer, with the master criminal Carl Peterson are rightly called 'rounds.' Geoffrey Household's unnamed hero in *Rogue Male* plays the blood sports of the gentry, as he hunts and is hunted by human adversaries. And most of Ian Fleming's tales have their game where Bond bests the villain, prefiguring the final struggle: golf in *Goldfinger*, bridge in *Moonraker*, baccarat in *Casino Royale*, skiing in *On Her Majesty's Secret Service*. In fact it could be argued that Fleming's greatest and not inconsiderable talent lies as a sports writer.

In another way, these thrillers are themselves a sort of game, a form which has its conventional players and established rules. Umberto Eco has analyzed the James Bond stories as a game where the reader knows the pieces, the rules, and the moves, and watches it unfold, taking pleasure in the game and its minor variations. The games in Fleming's tales are not only part of the suspense, prefiguring the final contest, but also a figure of the narrative itself.

Moreover, this concern for games is founded historically in the ethic of sportsmanship of the public schools of the late nineteenth and early twentieth century, an ethic that was disseminated and popularized by the 'school stories' of popular boys' weeklies, by a variety of popular fiction forms including the thriller, and by youth organizations like the Boy Scouts. The myth of the Newbolt man with his mystical loyalty to school, nation and Empire, and his philistine muscular Christianity, set the tone for the early thrillers of Childers, Buchan, and Sapper. It was an ethic that took the school cricket pitch, the celebrated playing fields of Eton, as a figure for social life, thus combining an institutional loyalty and reverence for hierarchical structures with a sense that social and political conflict was a game, to be played in a spirit of fairness, amateurism, and manliness.[29]

The crisis in the spy thriller that is marked by the passing of the romance of the heroic defense of the realm and by the arrival of the 'realistic' thriller parallels a crisis in this ethic of sportsmanship, and indeed invokes it. The irony of R. saying to Ashenden of a Mexican spy, 'He hasn't had the advantages of a public school education. His ideas of

playing the game are not quite the same as yours or mine,'
becomes evident through the course of Maugham's quiet
and desperate tales: for it becomes clear that the public
school ethic is only a mask for Ashenden's own sordid
though ineffectual games. No one is playing by the rules,
and, as we shall see at greater length later, this breakdown is
eventually condensed into the figure of Kim Philby.

If the concern for games in spy thrillers can be seen as a
figure for this larger ideological complex surrounding the
public school ethic of sportsmanship, an ideology which by
employing notions of amateurism and service both naturalizes the ruling elite and prescribes an ethic of service
throughout the social formation, we can recode the opposition between the romantic thriller and the realistic thriller.
For the romantic thriller involves the reasonably unproblematic staging of these games; and the so-called 'realistic'
thriller is the one which no longer plays by the rules, the one
where the rules are in doubt, where the crisis in the ideology
of good sports and honourable schoolboys is played out.

Formally, we can see that against the highly coded,
game-like structures of the romantic thriller, the codes of
realism still appear to be a demystifying, decoding operation; as we shall see, the rhetoric of the realists of the thriller
is entirely in this tone of breaking out of the highly coded –
and thus 'unrealistic' – worlds of the early thriller.

Another way of restating this distinction is that this
concern for breaking the rules – both the rules of the
ideological game of public school imperialism and of the
formal game of the conventional imperial thriller – is
manifested in a quite different ethical structure. All thrillers
are heavily coded by ethics, by the binary of good and evil:
but there is a difference between those that we might call
magical thrillers where there is a clear contest between
Good and Evil with a virtuous hero defeating an alien and
evil villain, and those that we might call existential thrillers
which play on a dialectic of good and evil overdetermined by
moral dilemmas, by moves from innocence to experience,
and by identity crises, the discovery in the double agent that
the self may be evil.

Finally, the significance of games points to a central distinction between the romantic and realistic thrillers, one which has little to do with fidelity to the 'real': the separation of work and leisure. For the thriller of games does not end with the crisis of the public school ideology. Its resurgence in the tales of Ian Fleming marks the combination of aspects of the older ideologies of Empire with the new access to mass sports and mass entertainment in the expansion of a new reified aspect of everyday life, 'leisure.' With the colonization of leisure through its mass industries – spectator sports, tourism, entertainment, and film – the thriller of games no longer features the aristocratic pleasures of blood sports and sailing. Rather these thrillers become both representations of mass leisure and instruction in its use. Thus Fleming's writing is infiltrated by the discourses of mass leisure: sports writing, tour guides, and advertising copy.

The realistic thriller, on the other hand, becomes increasingly the novel of work, and of a specific kind of work. For the modern stories of professional intelligence organizations like le Carré's 'Circus' are not really about spies at all; they are the representation and narration of the bureaucratic white-collar routine of information handling and office politics. Again the magical nature of the secret agent functions both as a wish-fulfillment, returning agency to a largely meaningless kind of work, and as an explanation of that work, a recognition of one's own lack of power. So, in the first case, George Smiley differs from the average government or corporate employee only in that his work has international repercussions; in the second case, there are the tragedies, or farces, of Leamas (*The Spy Who Came in from the Cold*) or Avery (*The Looking-Glass War*), betrayed by their own company in a game of which they were merely pawns. The class nature of the work represented also marks the shift in the audience of the 'realist' thriller to a white-collar base.

Thus the terms 'realism' and 'romance' do mark certain formal distinctions in the thriller, but those distinctions are rooted less in any fidelity to the 'real' than in divergent

attitudes to games, to established codes, to ethical structures, and to work and leisure.

2
Sport in a land flowing with strikes and profiteers

Empire and espionage

The spy thriller emerged near the turn of the century, during the 1890s and 1900s. A good deal of energy has been expended in determining the first spy novel, but the usual suspects – William Le Queux's *The Great War in England in 1897* (1893), E. Phillips Oppenheim's *The Mysterious Mr. Sabin* (1898), Rudyard Kipling's *Kim* (1901), Erskine Childers's *The Riddle of the Sands* (1903), or Joseph Conrad's *The Secret Agent* (1907) – are best seen not as candidates for the 'first' genuine spy novel but as signs of a break, markers of a shift in British popular fiction. This shift is part of what Stuart Hall has called 'the profound transformation in the culture of the popular classes which occurs between the 1880s and the 1920s . . . the period of what we might call the "social imperialist" crisis.' 'The more we look at it,' argues Hall, 'the more convinced we become that somewhere in this period lies the matrix of factors and problems from which *our* history – and our peculiar dilemmas – arise. Everything changes – not just a shift in the relations of forces but a reconstitution of the terrain of political struggle itself. It isn't just by chance that so many of the characteristic forms of what we now think of as "traditional" popular culture either emerge from or emerge in their distinctive modern form, in that period.'[1] Much of my account will be cast in terms of this crisis in social imperialism and imperialist culture; indeed, I will argue that the spy thriller is a symptom of this crisis and that the fortunes of the spy thriller are intimately tied to the task of managing and resolving this crisis in the popular imagination. But I will begin by trying to characterize three aspects of this break in the field of popular fiction: (1) the mutation of the adventure novel; (2) the emergence of the 'thriller' or 'shocker'; and (3) the emergence of espionage as a theme of increasing importance in thrillers.

The adventure story was the dominant genre in the popular fiction for men in Victorian England, ranging from the boys' stories of Mayne Reid, G.A. Henty, and R.M. Ballantyne to the tales of more established writers like Charles Kingsley, H. Rider Haggard and Robert Louis Stevenson. In what is the finest study of adventure stories to date, Martin Green argues convincingly that 'the adventure tales that formed the light reading of Englishmen for two hundred years and more after *Robinson Crusoe* were, in fact, the energizing myth of English imperialism.' The development of the adventure tale from Defoe to Kipling and Conrad is intertwined with the fortunes of Empire, but this relationship is mediated, according to Green, by two struggles within the literary system. The first struggle occurs within the adventure tale itself, which is caught between the 'modernist' adventure tale of Defoe with its emphasis on the hero's use of the tools and techniques of the modern world system and which represents the interests of the merchant caste, and the chivalric adventure of Scott which resurrects the heroes, virtues and exploits of earlier romance and represents the values of the aristomilitary caste. Green also shows how at the same time the ambivalence toward the Empire led to a gradual repression of the adventure tale from the 'literary' system which centered the domestic novel and relegated the adventure tale to the status of children's literature or popular entertainment. Green ends his account with the figures of Kipling and Conrad, two writers with contradictory relations to Empire, literature, and popular entertainment. After Kipling and Conrad, the Empire and the adventure tale were in crisis, and Green says in passing of the thrillers which followed:

> In prose, after Kipling came John Buchan; who was also a tremendously popular writer, and in terms of talent similar to Stevenson; that is, a man of great deftness, and craftsman-talent, but dedicated to adventure and soon repudiated by literature-as-a-system . . . At least in the world of literature one can say flatly that England after 1918 was unadventurous; men as serious as Defoe and Scott could no longer write adventures; and the men who could felt the moral support of their audience progressively withdrawn, so that the adventures grew more and more immoral, from Bulldog Drummond to James Bond . . . The adventure of imperialism had lost intellectual and moral credibility.[2]

The exhaustion of the adventure tale is thus one mark of this culture of the social imperialist crisis of 1880–1920; another mark is the rise of the 'thriller,' clearly non-literary and 'immoral,' a term to which I will return.

The 'thriller' or 'shocker' was not a representative of either the aristomilitary caste or the merchant caste (to use Green's terms), though it drew on conventions of both traditions. Rather it, along with the popular press which emerged at the same time, was a commercial product consumed by the working and lower-middle classes. And the thriller was not simply an exhausted, debased, and 'immoral' adventure tale. Rather, if the adventure tale was the energizing myth of English imperialism, the thriller became a compensatory myth of the crisis of imperialism.

One way in which this happened was through the emergence of espionage as an increasingly dominant theme. The early thriller was a mixture of many elements; an early handbook to writing thrillers defines them as 'any type of fiction . . . in which the sensational element preponderates . . . the detective story, the spy story, all stories of crime and intrigue, the underworld, and stories of thrilling adventure.'[3] Perhaps the greatest of the early thriller writers, Edgar Wallace, covered all of these and only rarely dealt with spies. The first spies were foreign agents, usually German but also French or Russian, and they appeared in the spate of thrillers which prophesied war. These tales uncovering plots to invade Britain and prophesying wars between Britain and France (and after the turn of the century between Britain and Germany) became a staple of Edwardian boys' story magazines and of the thriller in general.[4] The master of the invasion story was William Le Queux, whose *The Great War in England in 1897* (1893) was serialized in Harmsworth's weekly magazine *Answers*; in 1906, Harmsworth's new popular newspaper, the *Daily Mail*, published Le Queux's *The Invasion of 1910*. Le Queux's accounts of the ubiquitous German spy preparing the way for the invasion of the ill-prepared British isles was part of a wider 'spy fever' in Edwardian Britain, one in a series of moral panics which have been orchestrated around fears of espionage and which have included the Zinoviev letter of 1924, the atom bomb spies of the late 1940s, the Burgess–MacLean affair of 1951, the George Blake case in 1961, the Philby case of 1963 (revived by the press in 1967), and the Anthony Blunt affair of 1979. David French, in a study of this Edwardian spy fever, gives an illuminating account of the peculiar juxtapositions of fiction and reality in the course of a moral panic:

> Early in 1909 Le Queux published another book, *Spies for the Kaiser. Plotting the Downfall of England*. He wrote it with the specific intention of awakening the government and the public to the inadequacies of the British counter-intelligence system. His constant theme was that the east coast and London were swarming with German spies disguised as waiters, barbers, and tourists. They had orders to reconnoitre likely landing beaches, to list the resources of the countryside which might be useful to a hostile army, and to prepare to sabotage telephone, telegraph, and railway lines, bridges and water-mains.
>
> Almost as soon as the book was published he received a stream of letters telling him of the suspicious

behavior of German waiters, barbers and tourists in the vicinity of telephone, telegraph and railway lines, bridges and water-mains on the east coast and near London. The letters presented an almost exact mirror image of his book. He immediately sent them to [Lieutenant Colonel] Edmonds [of military operations counter-intelligence section] who used them to construct a picture of what he supposed was the German intelligence organization in Britain.[5]

So the espionage theme in the thriller is one part of this 'myth of the evil and ubiquitous German spy,' and this myth forms, as we will see, a part of the plots not only of the propaganda novelist Le Queux but of the diverse figures of Oppenheim, Childers and Buchan. Indeed, one of the marks of the transition from adventure story to thriller is this shift from an assertive, confident, and expansionist genre to an increasingly insular, even paranoid, genre stressing vigilance and protection against invasion, a shift that we might mark for convenience at the South African War.

What are we to make of this new spy thriller and of the ideologies of this moral panic, this spy fever? What can it tell us about Edwardian imperialist popular culture generally? Michael Blanch, in an essay on imperialism and popular culture, has argued that the notion of the *enemy outside* was one of the fundamental themes of imperialist culture at the time, linking youth organizations, schools, and the Empire Day movement; this leads him to conclude that 'imperialist and nationalist sentiment obtained real roots in working-class opinion.' Though I will not attempt to resolve the debate over the relation of imperialist ideologies to working- and lower-middle-class cultures, a brief sketch of the issues involved may aid in the interrogation of the thrillers of this period.

The argument that the English working class was jingoistic and supported the imperial adventures draws partly on a theoretical position which sees English workers, or a segment of them, as a labour aristocracy who had an objective stake in maintaining the Empire, and partly on an examination of Edwardian working-class culture. For example, after an analysis of various aspects of workers' culture, particularly the music hall, Gareth Stedman Jones concludes that 'if the working class did not actively promote the jingoism, there can be no doubt that it passively acquiesced to it.' Robert Roberts, in his account of life in Salford, says that the 'lower working class' clung to jingoism; and as examples he cites the popularity of Le Queux's novels, the influence of the chauvinistic campaigns against the Boers and the Germans by the *Daily Mail*, and the abundance of spy stories in popular speech: 'Germans who came here to "work", we were assured, could be spotted by a special button worn in the lapel. Each man had, we believed, sworn to serve Germany as a secret agent.'

A somewhat different view has been put forward by Richard Price, who, in a study of rowdyism against peace meetings, the election of 1906, and the incidence of volunteering for the army, concludes that workers were not extremely jingoistic and that the foot soldiers of popular imperialism, the instigators of the riots, were members of the lower-middle class, the growing army of black-coated workers, the clerks as well as teachers and poor clergymen: it was they who had the stake in the Empire and who were the main constituency of the popular press like the *Daily Mail* and *Answers*.[6]

A study of thrillers is not likely to resolve this debate about class and jingoism; however, a look at popular fiction will tell us that there is not an absolute divide in the Edwardian period between working-class culture and lower-middle-class culture – that the popular press, the story magazines, and the thrillers were read across the 'popular' classes and that this commercial culture, whether music hall, sports, boy scouts, Empire Day or fiction reading, was soaked with the figures and plots of Empire. Perhaps in these plots and figures and in the different ways in which they could be read we can unravel the culture of the social imperialist crisis.

Great impersonations

I will begin with the figure that entered the thriller and the popular imagination as part of the spy fever: the figure of the evil, ubiquitous, and brilliant German spy. This figure of the villain is particularly interesting since it was part of two quite different espionage formulas, the cloak-and-dagger formula and the amateur's defense of the realm formula. In the next section I will attempt to differentiate these formulas; at this point I am interested in what they share, that is, their concern for disguise and impersonation.

The books I will concentrate on are E. Phillips Oppenheim's *The Mysterious Mr. Sabin* (1898) and *The Great Impersonation* (1920), John Buchan's *The Thirty-Nine Steps* (1915), and Erskine Childers's *The Riddle of the Sands* (1903). E. Phillips Oppenheim was a rival to Edgar Wallace as the book factory of the age. A leather merchant from Leicester, he began to write in earnest in the mid-1890s and produced over 150 novels and books of short stories in the course of the next fifty years, novels of romance and espionage, country houses and the Riviera. His books are full of what Eric Ambler has called the 'early cloak-and-dagger stereotypes – the black-velveted seductress, the British secret service numbskull hero, the omnipotent spymaster.'[7] I have chosen two of his novels with a strong espionage theme: *The Mysterious Mr. Sabin*, his first real success, and *The Great Impersonation*, his greatest success and of all his novels the one which is most likely still to be read.

John Buchan and Erskine Childers were less typical of popular fiction writers; both were amateur novelists in a way. Childers was mainly a political figure: he had fought in South Africa and had written accounts of the war; later he fought for Irish home rule and served as de Valera's Minister of Propaganda. But in his one novel, in many ways a conventional war prophecy tract intended mainly as propaganda, he created a popular, long-lived and influential thriller.

John Buchan was a Scot who wrote adventure tales and

thrillers while pursuing an active business and political career that led from the colonial administration in South Africa after the war to an executive position at Reuters, to Parliament and finally to becoming Governor General of Canada. *The Thirty-Nine Steps* was written quickly and was intended as 'that elementary type of tale which Americans call the "dime novel" and which we know as the "shocker" – the romance where the incidents defy the probabilities, and just march inside the borders of the possible.' There is a story that Buchan began writing thrillers after becoming dissatisfied with those of Oppenheim and Wallace; in any case, he, like Childers, left behind many of the cloak-and-dagger conventions and wrested the thriller of espionage away from tales of diplomacy and high society by wedding it to the tale of imperial adventure. His basic plot was the hunt, a contest between hero and villain.

Despite their differences, however, all of these novels shared a central concern for the evil German masterspy and his disguises and impersonations. Mr. Sabin, the earliest, draws on the still imprecise nationality of the enemy outside; he is himself French but is selling the secrets of British coastal defenses to the Germans in order to gain support for a royalist restoration in France. The most extravagant and perhaps least interesting of all these villains, the 'mysterious' Mr. Sabin is a remarked-upon enigma from the first scene, and, though his murky past and diabolic plans are not known, as a foreigner of some sort he is suspected from the beginning.

The Great Impersonation begins with the German villain's plot to steal the identity of the dissipated Sir Everhard Dominey, lost in German West Africa; we then follow the success of Baron von Raggstein in impersonating Dominey back in England, a sort of mole among the English gentry. The ending is not, as we might expect, the revelation to the other characters of the false Dominey as the German spy Raggstein, but rather the turning of the tables on the reader, revealing that the false Dominey had been the real Dominey all along, deceiving his German spymasters in order to catch them. It is a reversal to which I will return.

In *The Riddle of the Sands*, the villain that the two amateur sailors, Davies and Carruthers, are tracking is the German Dollmann, ostensibly a businessman involved in a salvage operation off the Frisian Islands, but really, our heroes think, a spy who tried to run one of them aground. This seems a simple enough contest (though it is complicated by Davies's attraction to Dollmann's daughter); however, Davies also thinks that the German is really an Englishman in German service. Throughout the adventure the heroes are forced to doubt this: Dollmann certainly seems to be a German. But in the end they are proved right, and Dollmann turns out to be Lieutenant X—, R.N., an officer in Her Majesty's Navy who came to grief, 'disgrace, flight, exile,' and is now helping the Germans plan the invasion of Britain.

In *The Thirty-Nine Steps* there is another classic variant. Here the master German spy has no real name under his many pseudonyms; he is identified only as the old man with a young voice who can hood his eyes like a hawk. He and his gang, the Black Stone, chase Richard Hannay from London to Scotland because Hannay has, by accident, learned too much of their plot. When Hannay is able to put it all together, he turns the hunt around and goes after the Black Stone. Throughout the tale the man who can hood his eyes like a hawk appears under entirely innocent guises: as the bald archaeologist who shelters Hannay, as the First Sea Lord Allen, and as a typical middle-class suburbanite. Just as Davies and Carruthers are often led to believe that Dollmann is what he seems to be, so Hannay feels a fool arresting a game-playing English citizen as a German spy.

What is particularly interesting about *The Thirty-Nine Steps*, however, is that it formulates a theory of disguise, an explanation of impersonation, which is relevant to all of these stories. Hannay tells us that an Afrikaner scout, Peter Pienaar (who will turn up in some of the later adventures), had a theory about disguises:

> He said, barring absolute certainties like finger-prints, mere physical traits were very little use for

identification if the fugitive really knew his business. He laughed at things like dyed hair and false beards and such childish follies. The only thing that mattered was what Peter called 'atmosphere'. If a man could get into perfectly different surroundings from those in which he had been first observed, and – this is the important part – really play up to these surroundings and behave as if he had never been out of them, he would puzzle the cleverest detectives on earth.[8]

This is not only an accurate account of the man who could hood his eyes like a hawk and the principle behind the disguises that Hannay himself assumes in this and later adventures, but it is also an account of the other great impersonations in these early thrillers. The extravagant facial disguises we associate with Victorian melodrama (even with Sherlock Holmes) have given way to an ideal of impersonation. And this has both formal and ideological consequences.

The formal question is simply the necessity of producing a convincing villain. One of the distinguishing marks of the thriller is its villain, whether it be a master spy or criminal, a conspiracy or foreign secret service, or even one's own superiors. Unlike the adventure where the hero overcomes a series of trials, or the detective story where the question is the revelation of the guilty party, the thriller is based on paranoia and conspiracy: all of these events are part of a pattern which can be traced back to an evil source, a source which must not only be revealed but also be defeated. So a central formal problem of any thriller is to create a convincing and powerful villain as well as a convincing defeat of the villain. Genuine villains are not easily bested. In part this is accomplished by drawing on figures in the popular imagination, as we have seen in the case of the Edwardian spy fever. Julian Symons has pointed out that spy stories often followed the lines of contemporary military thinking, 'by which France was regarded as the prime danger to British security until the end of the nineteenth century, and was then replaced by Germany.'[9] One can see this sort of transition taking place in Oppenheim's *The Mysterious Mr. Sabin* when even the French villain is surprised to find that Germany and England, which he had thought were 'natural and inevitable allies,' are enemies, as Germany becomes the purchaser of the British naval secrets he is trying to obtain. One could follow the history of the thriller marking the changes in the nationality of the villains (though the Germans largely dominate from Bismarck's imperialism to the Cold War East Germans). But as our hasty description of the villains of Oppenheim, Childers, and Buchan already shows, their effectiveness derives from more than mere German nationality. First of all, there is an intertextual trumping, an explicit claim to greater verisimilitude in these stories than in previous romances. This trope is a common one but its frequency and often hackneyed character should not allow us to miss its power. It may be as simple as the offhand comment in *The Riddle of the Sands*, where Carruthers's encounter with a spy disabuses him of his received notions:

> I figured to myself one of those romantic gentlemen that one reads of in sixpenny magazines, with a Kodak in his tie-pin, a sketchbook in the lining of his coat, and a selection of disguises in his hand luggage.[10]

This same sort of operation is more elaborately worked in Buchan's *The Thirty-Nine Steps*. The tale of the Black Stone had originally been told to Hannay by Franklin Scudder and it was a tale of anarchists, financiers, and a 'subterranean movement going on . . . behind all the Governments and the armies.' After Scudder's death, Hannay decodes his notebook and discovers that this extravagant tale was a pack of lies; however, a true tale emerges, less extravagant but more threatening to England – the plot to steal the naval secrets. The trouble with Scudder was that he was too romantic: 'He had the artistic temperament and wanted a story to be better than God meant it to be.' But by displacing one plot by another, one villain by another, Buchan is able to produce a more convincing if no less implausible plot and villain.

But this formal trumping is, like the German nationality, only a fraction of the villain's power. The crucial operation comes in the type of impersonations depicted, the frightening interchangeability of German and British identities. It is not only the ability of the German agent to impersonate the English gentry but also the ability of an English naval officer to impersonate a German, or indeed the way an English gentleman can impersonate a German baron impersonating an English gentleman. The great impersonation seems at times no more than the face in the mirror. And we can see this figure as a recognition of the profound kinship of the two rival imperial powers, a recognition that is explicit in the explanation systems of some of the books. In *The Riddle of the Sands*, for example, Davies disgresses at length on the nature of the German empire, on its need for colonies, and on the role of sea power. In *The Mysterious Mr. Sabin*, Britain and Germany are spoken of as 'sister countries,' as 'cousins' sharing a 'common stock,' who are battling over colonies. This recognition of the kinship of British and German empires is much less evident in Buchan's books, but they were largely written during the First World War and are thus more determined on establishing the otherness of the 'Hun,' the 'Boche.'

But I think that the great impersonations of these thrillers have deeper roots than this sense of the kinship of rival empires. For the Germanic villains are not only the aristocrats of Oppenheim and the military men of Childers. It is interesting that Scudder's original tale in *The Thirty-Nine Steps*, the tale of the conspiracy of 'educated anarchists that make revolutions . . . and financiers who were playing for money,' is never entirely discredited in the novel; and this same conspiracy takes center stage in H.C. McNeile's ('Sapper') *Bull-dog Drummond* (1920), where master criminal Carl Peterson attempts to orchestrate a cabal of anarchists and financiers. What is interesting about these plots is the way that they are not directed against any one class as the villain (Sapper is as anti-capitalist as he is anti-worker) but at any vision of class as central to consciousness. Capital has no fatherland, Scudder tells us, and this is equally true of the aristocrats and gentry on the one hand, and of the anarchist and syndicalist workers on the other. These thrillers are an attempt to privilege a national consciousness over any class consciousness, and the threat comes from those who place class over nation. The peculiar interest of Oppenheim's novels is that he seems genuinely torn in sympathy; Mr. Sabin with his royalist plot to restore the monarchy in France may be unsuccessful in his villainous attempt to steal the secrets of British coastal defenses, but he succeeds in stealing the book from the young English hero, Lord Wolfenden. Sabin is Oppenheim's true hero and the book ends with his happiness in a new exile – for royalist plots are not to succeed – in America. Similarly, Oppenheim generates a tremendous amount of sympathy for his evil German spy, Baron von Raggstein, in his impersonation of Everhard Dominey in *The Great Impersonation*. Unable to simply destroy this heroic villain, he uses a brazen sleight of hand to tell us that Raggstein-Dominey was the English Dominey all along. It's elegant, not terribly convincing, and clearly demonstrates the true solidarity of Dominey and Raggstein, both gentlemen whether English or German.

The opposite case is Buchan's *The Thirty-Nine Steps*, an intensely nationalist tale, and the subsequent adventures of Richard Hannay. Here the theory of disguise is used in two quite different ways. The villains are able to move across national boundaries impersonating figures of their own class, whether workers or gentlemen. Hannay, on the other hand, uses Pienaar's tactics of disguise to move up and down the class structure while staying within and unifying the nationalities of the British Empire. So he can be a roadman one moment, a politician the next, a tramp, a mining engineer, a clubman.

Against the varieties of villainous internationalism figured in these great impersonations, Hannay's ventriloquism in acting the parts of the people of Britain and unifying them in a contest with aristocratic supra-national dynasties, international financiers, or 'tub thumpers of world revolution,' may be both a sign of and a reason for the effectiveness of these thrillers in constructing a popular 'national' readership, across and against class.

Amateurs

Having constructed a convincing villain, a spy who is alien, other, and yet through his impersonations proves to be something very close to oneself, the next task is to imagine a hero who can overcome this seeming omnipotence. Though this seems straightforward enough, it is not. Certainly in the case of Oppenheim, as we began to see in the previous section, a hero fails to emerge. In *The Mysterious Mr. Sabin*, it would appear to be the young Lord Wolfenden who will emerge as the hero; after all, it is his father who is on the brink of madness because Sabin is attempting to steal his secret papers, his mother who is being blackmailed by Sabin, and himself who is in love with Sabin's niece, the pretender to the French throne. And though he does win the hand of Princess Helène, he is unable to thwart Sabin's plot and indeed drops out of the story completely some way before the end. Rather Mr. Sabin's plot is summarily ended by an even more mysterious force, the High Council of the Nihilists; their representative tells Sabin to stop and he does. This transparent *deus ex machina* vitiates much of the interest of the story but is a symptom of Oppenheim's inability to imagine a hero. We see this again in *The Great Impersonation* where the *deus ex machina* is more success- ful but no less telling. The authorial reversal of the false Dominey into the real Dominey makes the villain the hero in one stroke; thus there is no need to imagine a separate and different hero who can conquer the cunning German. In- deed, the sympathies that have been aroused in the reader for the pretender are comfortably validated.

If we look back to Martin Green's distinction between the chivalric adventure and the mercantile adventure, I think we can begin to see the roots of Oppenheim's failure. For his own thorough attachment to the chivalric adventure — which is marked not by a genuine feudalism or aristocracy but by a peculiar combination of Gothic elements, descriptions of Society life and international playgrounds, and fantasies of royalist restorations – make his doomed Gothic villains far more convincing than any nationalist figure. So we must turn to the spy thriller marked by the tradition of the mercantile adventure, the thrillers of Buchan and Childers, to find this new hero, an amateur, a sportsman, an ordinary bourgeois, a Crusoe.

As Graham Greene put it, 'John Buchan was the first to realize the enormous dramatic value of adventure in familiar surroundings happening to unadventurous men, members of Parliament and members of the Athenaeum, lawyers and barristers, business men and minor peers.'[11] This hero is a sportsman, he hunts, fishes, and sails, and has imbibed the public school ethos of the cricket pitch. He is an amateur spy because the adventure breaks in on everyday life, 'the dismal but dignified routine of office, club, and chambers'; the stories of Childers, Buchan, and Sapper all begin with a man bored: 'Here I was, thirty-seven years old, sound in wind and limb, with enough money to have a good time, yawning my head off all day . . . the best bored man in the United Kingdom.'

Childers gives us two such heroes in *The Riddle of the Sands*: the bored and somewhat foppish Carruthers working in the Foreign Office in London in the summer and missing the fashionable society of the country, and the hard-working, somewhat dull and unfashionable Arthur Davies, a man connected with boats and the sea but not with yachting. In the adventure that follows, Carruthers finds his condescension toward Davies vanishing and his spine stiffening, as the two amateur sailors fall into the Great Game and save England from invasion.

Buchan's hero, Richard Hannay, is a mining engineer back from South Africa and Rhodesia who has adventure walk into his flat in dull London and finds himself pursued by both the police and a group of conspirators and foreign agents. Just as Carruthers and Davies prove themselves in contests on the sea, so Hannay uses his veldcraft to elude his pursuers across the wilds of Scotland. And Sapper's Bulldog Drummond advertises for adventure as 'Demobilised officer, finding peace incredibly tedious, would welcome diversion . . . Excitement essential.' He is a boxer and a member of the Junior Sports Club.

Such are the basic lineaments of the hero of the early spy thriller, the hero who is usually called the 'amateur' in typologies of the genre. These typologies usually set up an opposition between the amateur spies – the Hannays and the Drummonds – and the later professional spies – the James Bonds and George Smileys. Though this typology has its interest, particularly in terms of the role of work in the thriller, I would like to begin by distinguishing among several sorts of amateurs in the popular fiction of the early decades of the century, to try and account for their different meanings, and for the instability and contradictory character of the Buchan hero. The three amateurs I will look at briefly are the amateur spy, the amateur detective, and the gentleman outlaw.

All three of these figures must be seen not as fully formed and isolated archetypes but as counters in a character system which includes their opposite numbers; in order to determine the significance of their 'amateurism' we must look at the different sorts of professionalism to which they are opposed. For example, the amateur spy of the Buchan and Childers vintage is established against those professionals ordinarily responsible for national security, the diplomats. The novel of diplomacy is one of subtle and carefully orchestrated exchanges set against a polished background of Society manners and mores. These diplomats are major figures in the cloak-and-dagger tales and a late, transitional one is the figure of Prince Terniloff in Oppenheim's *The Great Impersonation*. Terniloff is very civilized, thoroughly unadventurous, and anxious to use diplomacy to cement his personal friendships with the English gentry into an international alliance between Germany and Britain. As he says at one point to the great impersonator himself: 'You know my one weakness, a weakness which in my younger days nearly drove me out of diplomacy. I detest espionage in every shape and form, even where it is necessary.' 'The school of diplomacy in which I have been brought up,' he says, 'tries to work without such ignoble means.'[12] But for all his good and peaceful intentions, Terniloff is shown to be naive and incompetent, a cat's-paw in a deeper and more ignoble game. If in Oppenheim and in the cloak-and-dagger tale there is a confrontation between the older novel of diplomacy and the new thriller of espionage, in the full-fledged thrillers the incompetence and naiveté of the professional diplomats is taken for granted. In the war-prophesying books, the entire narrative and ideological point is that the proper authorities are ignorant of the true dangers, and in Buchan's *The Thirty-Nine Steps*, when Hannay eventually does turn the case over to the Foreign Office, he has grave doubts as to their power: 'I told myself that it was sheer silly conceit, that four or five of the cleverest people living, with all the might of the British Empire at their back, had the job in hand . . . yet I was convinced that somehow I was needed to help this business through – that without me it would all go to blazes.'[13] And, of course, he is right.

The second amateur that we encounter in popular fiction of the period is the celebrated amateur detective of the classic detective story. This figure is usually assumed to be of an earlier vintage than the amateur spy (probably because of the Sherlock Holmes stories) and of a quite different lineage. However, LeRoy Panek has convincingly argued that, despite the line from Poe, Conan Doyle, and R. Austin Freeman, the detective stories of the so-called Golden Age (1914–40) are best understood as a reaction against the pre-war thrillers of Oppenheim, Wallace, and Buchan. Whereas the writers of thrillers were predominantly men from working- and lower-middle-class backgrounds, with casual educations, who often worked for the popular press (and had readers from the same background), the writers of detective stories were women and academics 'who gave talks about the detective story on the newly-founded BBC, who wrote articles on detection, who reviewed mystery novels, who – in short – remade the detective novel.' 'A basic premise of the new fiction,' argues Panek, 'was "this is a detective novel and not a thriller. It is not like Wallace, Oppenheim, Buchan or Le Queux."'[14] So the amateur created by the detective novel is a quite different amateur from that of the thriller: erudite rather than phili-stine, an intellectual rather than a sportsman, an eccentric rather than an ordinary man. The field of action has been reduced from the Empire to the country house, the criminal reduced from a master fiend to a member of the domestic circle. And the professional who is counterposed to this amateur is not the incompetent diplomat but the incom-petent policeman. We can see how the class dynamics which have often been noted about the writers and readers of thrillers and detective stories are worked out in the different meaning ascribed the amateur: in the first case the ordinary – though usually middle-class – hero proves the superior of the Society diplomats; in the other case, the leisured detec-tive outwits the working-class policeman.

But this is too simple an opposition and misses the contradictory and provisional nature of the amateur spy. For Buchan himself is an exception among thriller writers and the Richard Hannay of *The Thirty-Nine Steps* is an unstable creature. For the excitement of Hannay's flight and pursuit is its double nature: because of the murdered man found in his flat, he is running from both the foreign spies and the police (who are not bumbling incompetents). Once he is able to join forces with the government, half the tale is over and the other half – the capture of the man who stole the naval secrets – is merely a race against time. For Hannay to continue as a character – and Buchan was to write three more books about his adventures – he must either turn toward the government and become a profes-sional spy or he must turn away from the law and work independently. Hannay takes the first course and is sent out on missions by the government to protect the nation and Empire. Though he doesn't draw a salary, he is an agent of the Foreign Office and works in Germany and the Near East in *Greenmantle*, and infiltrates the pacifist community and the syndicalist workers of Clydeside in *Mr. Standfast*.

But this is not the main line of the thriller which, we will recall, includes many other themes besides espionage. Rather the main line of the thriller takes the tack of Richard

Hannay outside the law, the amateur sportsman fighting evil by means not always sanctioned, the gentleman outlaw. It is this line that Colin Watson has dubbed 'snobbery with violence';[15] it goes back to the Robin Hood of the 1890s, E.W. Hornung's Raffles, continues in Edgar Wallace's classic and sensational tale of 1905, *The Four Just Men*, and finds its most popular avatar in the 1930s with Leslie Charteris's the Saint. This tradition intersects with the spy thriller in a number of places, particularly in the figure of H.C. McNeile's Bull-dog Drummond. The Drummond stories come from the period immediately after the First World War and their plots are an attempt to resolve a host of ideological confusions. Drummond is, in a way, Richard Hannay demobilized, a fighter spoiling for a fight but without much sense of who or what to fight. In his advertisement for adventure placed in the newspapers he writes: 'Demobilised officer, finding peace incredibly tedious, would welcome diversion. Legitimate if possible; but crime, if of a comparatively humorous description, no objection. Excitement essential.' Drummond is a bundle of chauvinisms, hating Jews, Germans, and most other foreigners; he is a bully, a vigilante, and a thug, but the narrator covers his activities by telling us again and again that he is 'a sportsman and a gentleman,' and by saying that 'there are in England to-day quite a number of civilians who acknowledge only two rulers — the King and Hugh Drummond. And they would willingly die for either.'[16] This is the strain of the adventure tale that Martin Green finds 'immoral'; this is the bully-worship that Orwell finds pervading the boys' weeklies of the period.

The stories are simple contests between Drummond and his 'gang of boys' and a master criminal, Carl Peterson, and his gang of thugs. Peterson unites international financiers and international revolutionaries in a plot to create a Soviet Britain. Drummond foils each plot but never all the villains; they return for the next 'round' in book after book. The ideological framework which supports this makes little effort at coherence: as Drummond himself says, 'on the subject of Capital and Labour I am supremely ignorant.' We are never led to disagree with that statement. Rather the books may be summed up in the marvelous line from *Bull-dog Drummond*: 'Was it not sport in a land flowing with strikes and profiteers; sport such as his soul loved.'[17]

Bull-dog Drummond is usually taken as the nadir of the thriller, and is passed over quickly as the historian of the genre rushes from Buchan to Eric Ambler and Graham Greene. But to simply label Drummond 'immoral' is far from adequate. For Drummond is an important popular construction in a period of intensified class struggle, in a land which was indeed flowing with strikes and profiteers. Drummond's kin can be seen in the 'volunteers' who helped break the General Strike of 1926, and later in the supporters of Oswald Mosley's British Union of Fascists. But his popularity reached beyond these unseemly kin. Perhaps a more adequate framework has been suggested by Stuart Hall in his discussion of the language of the popular press: it is

> neither a pure construction of Fleet Street 'newspeak' nor is it the language which its working class readers actually speak. It is a highly complex species of linguistic *ventriloquism* in which the debased brutalism of popular journalism is skillfully combined and intricated with some elements of the directness and vivid particularity of working-class language. It cannot get by without preserving some element of its roots in a real vernacular – in the 'popular'. It wouldn't get very far unless it were capable of reshaping popular elements into a species of canned and neutralised demotic populism.[18]

Thus Drummond marshals a popular nationalism against aliens and subversive 'rotters' in what Hall has called 'authoritarian populism' in a way similar to the ventriloquism of Richard Hannay impersonating the different guises of the British 'people.' But it is worth noting not only the unmistakable authoritarian aspects of this, but also the utopian moment of the tale, the elements of a genuine if distorted populism. The Janus face of populism and nationalism is mirrored in the Janus face of the outlaw thriller; for if the outlaw thriller is a genre of vigilante attacks on other races and ethnic groups and a snobbish mystification of the rogue gentleman, it is also a genre of social banditry, of anti-authoritarian resistance, in marked contrast to the popular morality of the contemporary law-and-order genres which made heroes of policeman and detectives.[19]

Consider the tale that made Edgar Wallace famous in 1906, *The Four Just Men*. It is a story of the successful assassination of the British Foreign Secretary by a secret group of men of uncertain nationality who 'consider that justice as meted out here on Earth is inadequate, and have set themselves about correcting the law.'[20] In this case the Foreign Secretary wants to pass a bill which would extradite political refugees asylumed in Britain; the Four Just Men, in order to protect the leader of a 'great movement,' threaten the Foreign Secretary and, when he refuses to back down, ingeniously assassinate him in the midst of complete police protection. The Four Just Men are not caught, and the reader's sympathy remains with them throughout. Furthermore, Wallace, a *Daily Mail* journalist, offered a prize to readers who figured out the mystery of how the assassination was accomplished. One critic, William Vivian Butler, finds it 'a staggering fact that so many thousands of readers eagerly, and with never the slightest scruple, accepted Wallace's invitation to align themselves with his quartet of high-handed political murderers.'[21] (Interestingly, Butler does not find it staggering that so many readers, including himself, eagerly align themselves with Sapper's chauvinist thugs.)

The power of this Janus-faced outlaw, sometimes social bandit, sometimes vigilante, is such that it often leads to moral panics: one thinks of the outcry in the US in the early 1930s over the gangster films which led eventually to the antidote of the G-men films. And though such a marked public outcry was not aroused by the thriller, both Wallace and Sapper toned down their undisciplined heroes in the 1920s, to the point of aligning them with the police. Butler writes that 'on the whole the nineteen-twenties Wallace was a well-behaved citizen, firmly labelling crime as evil and criminals as wicked. The Just Men themselves were reduced to three and considerably tamed. ("The Three Just Men," comments the Assistant Commissioner in *Again the Three Just Men* (1928), "have become so respectable that we now give them police protection.").' Meanwhile, 'Sapper . . . disbanded the Black Gang, closed down that controversial establishment on the island west of Mull [a sort of private prison camp run by Drummond for anarchists and Bolsheviks], and brought Drummond & Co. into . . . close cahoots with the police.'[22] As we saw in the case of Richard Hannay, who went to work for the Foreign Office, the thriller's amateur outside the law was a contradictory and unstable creature.

3
Epitaph for an amateur

'He needed the money.' It was like an epitaph.
— Josef Vadassy, in Eric Ambler, *Epitaph for a Spy*

The simple art of spying

Hammett gave murder back to the kind of people who commit it for reasons, not just to provide a corpse; and with the means at hand, not hand-wrought dueling pistols, curare, and tropical fish . . . The realist in murder writes of a world in which gangsters can rule nations and almost rule cities . . .
— Raymond Chandler, 'The Simple Art of Murder' (1944)

[Mr. Ambler's] 'villains' are a strange and motley crew indeed. There are big business men and bankers; the cheap scum of the low cafés of the ancient Continental cities; the professional, suave, well-heeled gangsters whom we have learned to recognize as the incipient chiefs of Gestapos and fascist conspiracies. In brief, they are not only real people, they are actually the kind of people who have generated violence and evil in the Europe of our time.
— Alfred Hitchcock, Introduction to Eric Ambler Omnibus, *Intrigue* (1943)

If the history of forms and genres is to serve as a mediator between individual texts and the larger history of the social formation, then the moments of transformation, the moments when a new configuration of formulas and conventions comes to dominate the genre, is of particular significance. For at these moments we can begin to read the differences between texts as symbolic acts, and can see the reconstitution of the elements of the genre not only as a matter of formal variation but as a symptom of changes in the reading public and the historical situation. In the justifications of the new practice, in the new aesthetic ideology, one can see the marks of general ideological conflict, the attempt to resolve nagging antinomies, and to construct a new effect of reality because an earlier one no longer seems 'natural' or convincing.

In the history of the thriller, a central mutation in the genre occurs with the early stories of Eric Ambler and Graham Greene in the 1930s. Contemporary reviewers commented on the emergence of a new and, to their mind, more serious thriller: as Anthony Boucher wrote, 'At last Ambler came; and from his *Uncommon Danger* (1937) we may date the transfiguration of the spy story . . . Ambler showed that human characterization, good prose, political intelligence, and above all a meticulously detailed realism, far from getting in the way of intricate spy adventures, can strengthen them and raise them to a new plane.' Similarly, James Sandoe wrote that 'Eric Ambler took over the form in a sad state of disrepair. Buchan had forsaken it, largely, and the heavy dominance of E. Phillips Oppenheim had grown excessively tedious. Ambler took the spy story by the scruff of its well-washed neck, whipped the monocle out of its astonished eye and pushed it down among people, away from the world of diplomatic mummies.'[1]

More recent accounts of this shift, including Ambler's own account, tend to name W. Somerset Maugham's novel *Ashenden* (1928) as the initial text responsible for the breakthrough; but the crystallization of a new sort of spy novel occurs in Ambler's six pre-war novels (1936–40) and in Greene's 'entertainments' of the 1930s. We might also include the spy stories of Compton Mackenzie, the early novels of Helen MacInnes, and Peter Cheyney's 'Dark' series to indicate that the shift away from the models of Sapper and Oppenheim was a general one and not limited to the peculiar genius of Eric Ambler.

However, we must also realize throughout that the spy novel is only part of the popular thrillers of the 1930s, and the tradition of the gentleman outlaw is maintained through the period by Dennis Wheatley, John Creasey (the Toff, the Baron), and, most prominently, Leslie Charteris (the Saint). These writers were published in the twopenny weekly *The Thriller*, which lasted from 1929 to 1940, and were then reprinted in the Hodder & Stoughton Yellow Jackets.

The shift marked by Ambler and Greene was self-conscious and was accompanied by various justifications – what we might call, following Terry Eagleton, an aesthetic ideology, a set of unconscious values and conscious projects that establish a certain definition of aesthetic value and the artist's role. In the case of Ambler, Greene and Maugham, what we might call the 'serious thriller,' this aesthetic had three basic components: 'realism,' moral and literary seriousness, and popular front politics. In what follows I want to briefly outline these aspects of the aesthetic of the serious thriller, and then look at how they are manifested in the stories – first, in the change in the amateur hero, and second, in the new relation between the narrator and the characters.

The serious thriller began with a contradictory project: it combined a dissatisfaction with earlier thrillers with a faith in the possibilities and indeed the peculiar relevance of the thriller, a sense that the thrillers of Buchan and Oppenheim, the Yellow Jackets of the 1920s, were no longer convincing, together with a conviction that the thriller had a certain privileged relation to the modern world. Thus Graham Greene writes:

An early hero of mine was John Buchan, but when I reopened his books I found I could no longer get the same pleasure from the adventures of Richard Hannay. More than the dialogue and the situation had dated:

the moral climate was no longer that of my boyhood. Patriotism had lost its appeal, even for a schoolboy, at Passchendaele, and the Empire brought first to mind the Beaverbrook Crusader, while it was difficult, during the years of the Depression, to believe in the high purposes of the City of London or of the British Constitution. The hunger marchers seemed more real than the politicians. It was no longer a Buchan world. The hunted man of *This Gun for Hire*, which I now began to write, was Raven, not Hannay: a man out to revenge himself for all the dirty tricks of life, not to save his country.[2]

However, if it was no longer a Buchan world, it was still a world of the thriller, as Arthur Rowe says in Greene's *The Ministry of Fear*:

It sounds like a thriller, doesn't it, but the thrillers are like life . . . You used to laugh at the books Miss Savage read — about spies, and murders, and violence, and wild motor-car chases, but dear, that's real life . . . The world has been remade by William Le Queux.[3]

The serious thriller is an attempt to resolve this contradiction, this sense that the extremity of violence and melodrama in the thriller offers a way of seeing despite the anachronism of the earlier heroic thrillers and their worlds.

The first part of the solution is named 'realism.' Just as Hitchcock writes that Ambler's books are made of the 'material of reality,' so Ambler sees Maugham's breakthrough as one towards realism. Realism functions with different meanings and in different ways in many aesthetics; here we can find at least two meanings. First, it connotes a certain view of reality where violence and brutality are fundamental, where the decorums of 'civilized' behavior are but a thin veil over naked power relations, where nations and empires are less the expression of a civilizing mission than the mask for exploitation, and where the ethic of sportsmanship and the game is at best an anachronism and at worst a mystification. The second meaning encompasses the formal conventions which produce the effect of this 'reality': the meticulous representation of physical violence, the depiction of the brutality and seediness of ordinary life, a dialogue composed of abrupt, tough slang, and melodramatic plots that dramatize the eruption of the real – the violent – into everyday life. Though this realism shares much with the naturalist aesthetic, it departs from naturalism's 'scientific' mission of a massive 'natural history of society' to focus on the briefer and more melodramatic moral dilemma of the hero in an extreme situation. This 'realism' also shares much with the 'realism' of the American hard-boiled novels of the late 1920s and 1930s, an aesthetic ideology codified in Raymond Chandler's essay 'The Simple Art of Murder.' As we will see, the hard-boiled aesthetic had substantial and contradictory effects on the subsequent history of the thriller.

A second aspect of the thriller of Ambler and Greene is its 'seriousness.' Again this has a semantic as well as a formal nature. It manifests itself first as a concern for moral dilemmas, for the ambiguities and uncertainties of ethical behavior, and for the questions of loyalty and betrayal. Unlike earlier thrillers, with their straightforward moral schema which designated hero and villain as good and evil and authorized the actions of the hero by the transcendent value of the nation and his sporting observance of the rules of the game, the 'serious' thriller takes as its subject the uncertainty of the authority for the protagonist's actions, the lack of a clear-cut 'good,' and the ensuing issues of innocence and experience, of identity and point of view.

But this moral seriousness is accompanied by a 'literary' seriousness which was not present in the earlier thrillers. This is not simply to say that the thrillers of the 1930s are better written than those of Buchan and Sapper: some are and some clearly are not. Rather the intention of this aesthetic ideology is to write thrillers which are marked by the 'literary' as it was defined in the early twentieth century: by an emphasis on unity of character rather than unity of plot, by the narrative figuring of the writer (Maugham's Ashenden and Ambler's Latimer are both writers) and the dilemmas of storytelling, and, perhaps crucially, by the concern for the issue of point of view, the relation between narrator and character, the concern for the way the story is learned and told. This formal concern for point of view is, I hope to show, intimately connected to the moral serious-ness of these thrillers.

This literary seriousness can also be seen in the type of writers dominating the thriller. Whereas the early thriller was dominated by the book factories like Wallace and Oppenheim on the one hand, and amateur novelists with business or political careers like Childers and Buchan on the other, the thrillers of the 1930s were often written by literary writers using the conventions of the thriller on occasion (Maugham, Greene, Mackenzie). There were, to be sure, continuities; Ambler's first contract was with Hod-der & Stoughton and his early novels appeared as Yellow Jackets. But by the end of World War II, we have passed from the age of Edgar Wallace to the age of Graham Greene, the period when the circulating libraries of Boots and W.H. Smith were in decline and were being replaced by the public library as the main consumer of fiction and the mainstay of the middlebrow novel. There also seems to have been a shift in the readership of spy thrillers from the earlier working-class/lower-middle-class configuration to a clerical/service/professional-managerial class configuration, a shift marked by and perhaps due to this growing 'literariness.' In a provocative analysis of the 'middlebrow' novel of the 1930s, the 'realist' novel with an ambiguous relation to the 'literary,' the Birmingham Centre's English Studies Group has argued that the reader of the middlebrow novel is characteristically 'interpellated in the position of the author or narrative "point-of-view".' The 'lowbrow' or mass form-ulaic novel 'interpellates' or situates its reader in a posi-tion of identification with one or more characters, and the 'highbrow' or modernist novel situates the reader in the position of literature itself. These various situations are tied, the English Studies Group argue, to the different educations of different classes and reading publics in the school system. Though they admit that this is a somewhat schematic ideal type, it certainly has the merit of constructing a mediation between the formal mechanisms of the text – in our case the growing importance of point of view in the thriller – and the shift in the reading public.[4]

Finally, this aesthetic is constituted by a popular front politics, what we might call an anti-fascist aesthetic. Here is Eric Ambler's account of his early novels:

> *having failed* at playwriting, *having failed* as a song-writer, *failed* as an engineer, I looked around for something I could change and decided it was the thriller-spy story . . . The detective story genre had been worked over and worked over, but no one had looked at the thriller. It was still a dirty word. So I decided to intellectualize it, insofar as I was able. It wasn't very far then, but it was sufficient. I changed the genre and couldn't write the books fast enough . . . Sapper was writing solid right wing. He was an out-right fascist. He even had his heroes dressed in black shirts. Buchan was an establishment figure, so club and fuddy-duddy and I decided to turn that upside down and make the heroes left wing and popular front figures.[5]

One might object that this is not part of Ambler's aesthetic: surely this ought to be considered as part of Ambler's political opinions. However, there are a few reasons for treating Ambler's (and Greene's) popular front anti-fascism as essentially an aesthetic position. First, this anti-fascism marks Ambler's novels much more than it seems to mark his politics, which remain relatively unfocused. But more substantially, it manifests itself in formal ways. As Martin Green has suggested, an ironic and critical stance toward the Empire often appeared as an ironic stance toward the adventure genre, toward any simple heroism or romance, particularly in the writers close to the literary system (Conrad, Maugham, Greene). So the anti-fascism of the thriller enters not only as a set of authorial opinions, but as a reversal of the earlier codings of heroes and villains, over-turning not only Sapper and his blackshirts but Conrad and his counter-revolutionary spy novels as well. For Conrad is as pervasive an influence on the serious thriller as is Sapper or Buchan.

Finally, the 'realism' of these thrillers is intertwined with their anti-fascism. For the representation of violence as the *real*, and the melodrama constructed around the intrusion of violence into everyday life, are both situated by a semantic opposition of humanity/brutality, a binary that might be characterized as the focal point of an anti-fascist aesthetic. But this 'realism' has another side, which is figured in the contradictory influence of the 'Yank mags,' the American hard-boiled pulp magazines. We have noted the parallel between Ambler's project and that of Hammett and Chandler, but the American hard-boiled mode was also picked up in Britain by such writers as Peter Cheyney and James Hadley Chase, whose depictions of violence were combined with the opinions of a Sapper into what George Orwell, in one of his famous attacks on popular fiction, called 'bully-worship and the cult of violence.'[6] For the simple good/evil schema of the earlier thriller, they substituted one where there was 'no moral dividing line between "sleuth" and criminal.'[7] So in the same way that Ambler labels Sapper a fascist, Orwell characterizes Chase as a fascist (as for Cheyney, he was an ardent supporter of Oswald Mosley's British Union of Fascists):

> Several people, after reading Chase's *No Orchids for Miss Blandish*, have remarked to me, 'It's pure Fascism.' This is a correct description, although the book has not the smallest connection with politics and very little with social or economic problems. It has merely the same relation to Fascism as, say, Trollope's novels have to nineteenth century capitalism. It is a day dream appropriate to a totalitarian age.[8]

We can see this fascist aesthetic which heroizes brutality as, in a way, the occasion for and the obverse of the anti-fascist one of Ambler. Thus the sign of Ambler's anti-fascism lies less in a specific political position than in the centrality of the figure of a rubber truncheon, the *Totschläger* or 'beater-to-death' of Nazi Germany.

Following this brief account of the new aesthetic of these thrillers of the 1930s, their simple art of spying, I will turn to look more closely at the stories that they tell, the stories of innocents abroad, and then at the way they tell those stories, under Western eyes.

Innocents abroad

> . . . loss of innocence. It's the only thing I've ever written.
>
> – Eric Ambler

There is no series character in the early novels of Eric Ambler, no Richard Hannay or James Bond. But Ambler produced a type, a recurring figure which is probably as clearly defined in the popular imagination as Hannay or Bond: the innocent abroad. The names change – Henry Barstow in *The Dark Frontier* (1936), Desmond Kenton in *Uncommon Danger* (1937), Josef Vadassy (a non-British version) in *Epitaph for a Spy* (1938), Nicolas Marlow in *Cause for Alarm* (1938), Charles Latimer in *The Mask of Dimitrios* (1939), and Winston Graham in *Journey into Fear* (1940) – but the lineaments are recognizable: an educated, middle-class man (a journalist, teacher, engineer) travelling for business or pleasure on the Continent who accidentally gets caught up in a low and sinister game (no longer the Great Game) of spies, informers, and thugs. He is innocent both in the sense of not being guilty, and in the sense of being naive. He is an amateur spy, but not the sort of enthusiastic and willing amateur that Hannay is; rather he is an incompetent and inexperienced amateur in a world of professionals. This figure is not found only in Ambler: the young Oxford couple in Helen MacInnes's first novel, *Above Suspicion* (1941), are a more heroic version and the first of many innocents in her work; we see him too in Greene's Arthur Rowe of *The Ministry of Fear* (1943) and Rollo Martins of *The Third Man* (1950); and the entangled innocent is a favorite character of Hitchcock's film thrillers, particularly *The Lady Vanishes* (1938).

The plots which entangle the Ambler innocent are of two main types, the hunted man and the trapped man. In the first, an incident leads to the protagonist being wanted by the police as well as by the professional spies, and he has to flee, often in a manner reminiscent of the Richard Hannay of *The Thirty-Nine Steps*, adopting disguises, climbing through mountain passes, and avoiding passport inspectors on trains. In the trapped man plot, the innocent is in a situation that can't be escaped – Graham on the steamer, Vadassy in the hotel – and must play out the desperate game, trying to flush out the spy who threatens him from among the seemingly innocent body of passengers or guests.

I want to look at this innocent, the nature of his innocence, and the way it is lost, beginning with the relation of this innocent to the amateurs that preceded him, a relation which is staged by both Maugham and Ambler. For both Maugham and Ambler begin by showing that the tales of the heroic and competent amateur are themselves innocent. Maugham's Ashenden is clearly a transitional figure between the Buchan amateur and the Ambler innocent. Like Hannay, Ashenden is an amateur brought in to defend the nation; but the incidents (one could hardly call them adventures) that involve him leave him more the pawn than the agent of events, a failure in the attempt to change history. The real adventure, the one he is meant to prevent, happens off-stage; that, of course, is the Russian Revolution and we will return later to its significance in the stories.

Ambler is even more explicit on his relation to the earlier amateur heroes and two of his stories in large part stage the fate of the amateur. In his first novel, *The Dark Frontier* (1936), Ambler tells the story of Henry Barstow, a methodical and orderly scientist who, as a result of a car accident, awakes to`think he is the storybook hero Conway Carruthers, Dept. Y: 'free from the fears and the vanities, the blunderings and shortcomings of ordinary men, he was of that illustrious company which numbers Sherlock Holmes, Raffles, Arsène Lupin, Bull-dog Drummond, and Sexton

Blake among its members.' His name, we might note, is taken from one of the heroes of *The Riddle of the Sands*. As Carruthers, he takes on the identity of a mild-mannered English physicist, Henry Barstow, and goes to the Eastern European country of Ixania to prevent the development of an atomic bomb and to help a peasant revolution. By the end he has reverted back to himself (Barstow), and has no memory of anything after the car accident. Our narrator supplies some tongue-in-cheek documentation on cases of dual personality to explain the exploits of Barstow/ Carruthers. The entire tale is a gentle satire of the conventions of the heroic spy as Carruthers succumbs to the wiles of a seductive woman spy, gets out of impossible jams, and saves the Ruritanian nation of Ixania. The second half of the book is narrated by the American journalist Casey, who helps Carruthers/Barstow and is continually amazed by him:

> In the everyday affairs of life he was a nonentity, a blur . . . It was only in moments of crisis that he became an individual. At such moments he was immense . . . I invariably found myself amazed by the way in which sheer luck had converted what, in cold blood, seemed asinine decisions into strokes of genius . . . Carruthers had a way of making you behave and think like a dime novel.

However, undergridding this tale is the quite serious inability of the apolitical and naive physicist Barstow to deal with the realities of commercial armaments competition. Just before his car accident, Barstow had been offered the position of technical adviser to the armaments producer Cator & Bliss, in order to steal the atomic secrets of the government of Ixania. Barstow is appalled both by the Ixanian perversion of science to destruction and by Cator & Bliss's desire to own the atomic secrets exclusively: 'I am hoping,' he says, 'that this is all a very unpleasant dream and that I shall soon wake up.'[9] His inability to act – for he turns down Cator & Bliss and tries to forget the entire affair – is followed by the car accident and his magical transformation into Conway Carruthers, the man who does act and foils the plots of both the Ixanian government and Cator & Bliss. Though Barstow's dilemma will recur in later Ambler novels, the Carruthers solution is clearly inadequate: such a hero is a mere sport.

If *The Dark Frontier* satirizes the amateurs of Buchan, Childers, and Sapper, *The Mask of Dimitrios* (1939) takes on a different amateur, the cool and rational detective of the classical country house mystery. Charles Latimer, one of the 'great army of university professors who write detective novels in their spare time,' author of *A Bloody Shovel, Murder's Arms*, and *No Doornail This*, goes abroad to write and meets one of his readers, the Turkish policeman Colonel Haki. After telling Latimer of his own dismal plot for a *roman policier*, Haki begins to tell him the sordid and inartistic story of a *real* murderer, Dimitrios Makropoulos, whose body has just been fished out of the Bosphorus. Latimer decides to put together the biography of this Dimitrios, and finds the loose ends far from tied up and the detective – himself – far from invulnerable. When Latimer first finds himself facing a gun, the narrator tells us that 'in only one of his books, *Murder's Arms*, had Latimer handled a situation in which one of the characters had been menaced by a murderer with a revolver' and he had been uneasy with that piece of melodrama.[20] But the entire of *The Mask of Dimitrios* is a coming to terms with the real melodrama that Latimer's fictions with their rules and decorums carefully exclude.

Just as the essential innocence and naiveté of the tales of the amateur is revealed by crossing the boundaries that circumscribe the genre, by showing the chaos that reigns just outside the frontiers of the rules of the game, so this crossing of boundaries and frontiers may be taken as the characteristic way the protagonist of the Ambler tale discovers or loses his innocence. There are a number of these frontiers, but they follow the pattern set in the first novel, *The Dark Frontier*: 'One half of your brain became an inspired reasoning machine, while the other wandered over dark frontiers into strange countries where adventure,

romance, and sudden death lay in wait for the traveller . . .'
The frontier referred to here is that into daydreaming, but
one could take the crossing of a frontier as a condensation
of several levels and types of action in the novels: the
frontier between consciousness and unconsciousness which
is crossed not only in sleep and daydreaming but in the event
of being slugged on the head; the frontier between work and
holiday which motivates several of the plots (or the reverse
one between unemployment and a new job that sets *Cause
for Alarm* in motion); and the actual frontiers between the
European states, the crossing of which entails the anxiety
about passports, identity papers, and customs searches, the
source of much of the suspense in an Ambler novel.

The crossing of any and all of these frontiers generates the
experience of the *real* which punctures the protagonist's
carefully protected innocence. This innocence proves to be
of several varieties, concerning violence, history, Englishness, and knowledge. But before looking at these it is worth
noting a significant absence: sexuality. Aside from the mild
anxiety generated in the Ambler Englishman by a variety of
Continental countesses and dancers or by the hint of
homosexuality, romance plays but a small part in these tales
and sexuality an even smaller one.

Rather it is the experience of violence which is graphically
described and which marks the hero's loss of innocence. It is
the intrusion of melodrama into ordinary life, if we accept
for a moment Raymond Chandler's definition of melodrama as 'an exaggeration of violence and fear beyond what
one normally experiences.' Violence emerges in the Ambler
world in a number of ways: in the fear generated by an
'accidental' assault, in the arbitrariness of local policemen
and minor customs officials who deprive one of one's
papers and thus of one's mobility and identity, in the chance
meeting on a train, in the necessary deals of the business
world, legitimate and illegitimate. Its effect in the metaphysic of the serious thriller is to mark out the thin layer of
civilization and show its contingency: danger, fear, and
violence were 'there just the same, waiting to make non-
sense of all your comfortable ideas about your relations

with time and chance, ready to remind you – in case you had forgotten – that civilization was a word and that you still lived in the jungle.'[11]

The epitome of this violence is systematic torture, the truncheon-wielding thug out to get information: 'authority,' Ambler has said in an interview, 'is a dumb beast . . . It's not grandiose figures sitting behind huge baroque desks with shaded light . . . It's some dingy little figure with delusions of grandeur.' And despite the fact that this dumb beast is often figured as a German or Italian fascist, it can often look like Bull-dog Drummond; one of the more memorable thugs is Captain Mailler, who 'was in the Black-and-Tans, and was also, at one time, the only professional strike-breaker in America with an English public school education.' The confrontation with this systematic and legitimate violence leads to the modest sort of heroism the Ambler character has, the refusal to compromise or give in, the assertion of 'humanity' against 'brutality.' Whatever other wavering occurs over money, patriotism, or principle, there is no compromise with the truncheon. As the journalist Kenton says in his speech to his torturers:

> You made the mistake of supposing that I could be successfully intimidated. It's not just a struggle between Fascism and Communism, or between any other – isms! It's between the free human spirit and the stupid, fumbling, brutish forces of the primeval swamp – and that, Colonel, means you and your kind.

The language of these frequent meditations by narrator or character on fear and violence is marked by the oppositions civilization/jungle, humanity/brutality, human spirit/ primeval swamp: oppositions which are drawn from an earlier popular rhetoric of the Empire's 'civilizing mission' and now recast into an anti-fascist rhetoric. The dark frontier of adventure and romance which is crossed on the border of sleep and wakefulness was once the colonial frontier; it is now a European frontier.[12]

The crossing of this frontier demonstrates the innocence not only of the protagonist but of the English generally, aptly epitomized by an exchange in Hitchcock's *The Lady Vanishes*. As the plot to abduct Miss Froy begins to come to light as an *official* one, the passengers on the train must decide whether to resist the German officials about to board the train. The Basil Radford character, Charters, a proper and skeptical Britisher, says when he hears of the plot, 'Things like that just don't happen.' To which Miss Froy replies, 'We're not in England now.' That we are no longer in England, no longer subject to fair play, non-violence, and rational justice, is something that all of Ambler's characters must learn. And this may lead to a heightened sense of 'Englishness,' as it does for the commercial traveller in *Uncommon Danger* who shelters Kenton from the police without question because Kenton is a Britisher. And one could, indeed, see this characteristic story of the innocent abroad entrapped in a continent of violence as a way of narrating the recognition by the British that, for all their 'non-ideological' tradition and character, they were entangled in the violent struggles of the ideologies of fascism and communism on the Continent.

But the price of recognition for Ambler's main characters (unlike those in *The Lady Vanishes* or in Helen MacInnes's tales) is the realization that 'England' no longer exists, that it is not uninvolved, that, though it may be naive, it is not innocent. As the plot unravels, the lines go back to the City of London. For just as the 'man who could hood his eyes like a hawk' lies behind the myriad villains of Buchan, and as Carl Peterson, master criminal, lies behind the many sparring partners of Bull-dog Drummond in the tales of Sapper, so there is a shadowy character behind the scenes of the early Ambler novel: Cator & Bliss, the armaments producer.

In an essay on class in contemporary popular culture, Frederic Jameson has argued that

> in order for genuine class consciousness to be possible, we have to begin to sense the abstract truth of class through the tangible medium of daily life in vivid and experiential ways, and to say that class structure is

becoming representable means that we now have gone
beyond mere abstract understanding and entered that
whole area of personal fantasy, collective storytelling,
narrative figurability . . . To become figurable – that is
to say, visible in the first place, accessible to our
imaginations – the classes have to be able to become in
some sense characters in their own right.

He goes on to argue that with the emergence of the 'multinational corporation' as a character in the popular imagination in the 1970s, 'capitalism becomes objectified and
dramatized as an actor and as a subject of history with an
allegorical intensity and simplicity that had not been the
case since the 1930s.'[13] And if one were to look at the
moments when capitalism has become figurable and at the
shapes that it has assumed, the figure of the armaments
manufacturer in the 1930s emerges as one of the clearest
and most intense. We are a long way from the confused
unions of international financiers and working-class syndi-
calists that we find in Sapper and from the royalist restoration plots of Oppenheim when we read of the corporations
of Ambler – (Cator & Bliss, Pan-Eurasian Petroleum, the
Eurasian Credit Trust) – and of Greene – Sir Marcus's
Midland Steel (with its armaments interests in *A Gun for
Sale*, 1936) and the Benditch Colliery Company in *The
Confidential Agent* (1939). These emerge as a testament
both to the new figurability of capitalism after the General
Strike and the Depression and to the thriller's formal re-
quirement of a convincing and unified villain.

However, though the armaments firm looms in the background as a force impinging on the lives of many innocents,
its face appears through various displacements. Only in the
brief and relatively unsuccessful prologue to *Uncommon
Danger* does the corporation appear as a board of human
directors in the City. More often, the corporation is visible
in its effects, and is figured by those intermediaries who
carry out the plots, the hired guns. The inadequacy of the
detective story is that it ends when it reveals the murderer;
but as Colonel Haki tells Latimer, 'The important thing to

know about an assassination or an attempted assassination is not who fired the shot, but who paid for the bullet.'[14] In Graham Greene's *A Gun for Sale*, this is indeed the movement of the narrative, from Raven, the hired gun, to Sir Marcus. But guilt is perhaps too easily fixed here, and thus becomes a pretext to the metaphysical questions of guilt and betrayal that entwine the hare-lipped assassin Raven to the showgirl Anne, and allow Greene to superimpose a Christian parable over a thriller, an 'entertainment.'

In Ambler's narratives there is no straight line from hired gun to employer, and the stories center on the intermediaries, 'the professionals, the *entrepreneurs*, the links between the business men, the politicians who desire the end but are afraid of the means, and the fanatics, the idealists who are prepared to die for their convictions.'[15] These characters – Dimitrios, Vagas, Saridza – have all worked for Cator & Bliss, and they seduce, blackmail, and bully the English innocents into the jungle. They are freelance spies, not organization men; and they are not amateurs: they need the money.

They are of uncertain nationality and, like the villains of earlier thrillers, oppose any nationalism. 'One should not,' one of these entrepreneurs of information, Vagas, says, 'allow one's patriotism to interfere with business. Patriotism is for the *café*. One should leave it behind with one's tip to the waiter.'[16] Business has no frontiers, it crosses national boundaries with the best papers money can buy, and it crosses the frontier of the legal and illegal without regard.

But the recognition and demystification of innocence goes further than the realization that the fascist brutes the hero encounters on the Continent have lines running back to London, that the English 'innocence' of ideology is merely a commitment to the most profitable investment. Rather the stories continue to explore the dilemma that Barstow was able to repress only by magically transforming himself into a storybook hero, the recognition of one's own complicity, the recognition that the professors, engineers, and commercial travellers that populate the Ambler world are themselves hired guns. To each of them the moment comes when they want to pull back, when they want to say, as Nicolas Marlow does, 'But that would make me a spy,' and they are told, 'in tones of infinite contempt,' 'My dear Marlow, you already *are* a spy.'[17]

Here the protagonists cross a frontier to find that their innocence lies in thinking of their knowledge as innocent. 'I'm not a business man. I'm an engineer,' Marlow maintains, a technician pure and simple who can't see 'what possible connexion there could be between the Rome-Berlin axis and machine tools.' Or as one of Ambler's cynical and ironic narrators says:

> For Graham a gun was a series of mathematical expressions resolved in such a way as to enable one man, by touching a button, to project an armour-piercing shell so that it hit a target several miles away plumb in the middle. It was a piece of machinery no more and no less significant than a vacuum cleaner or a bacon slicer. It had no nationality and no loyalties. It was neither awe-inspiring nor symbolic of anything except the owner's ability to pay for it. His interest in the men who had to fire the products of his skill as in the men who had to suffer their fire (and, thanks to his employers' tireless internationalism, the same sets of men often had to do both) had always been detached . . .
>
> But this revolver was different. It wasn't impersonal. There was a relationship between it and the human body. It had, perhaps, an effective range of twenty-five yards or less. That meant that you could see the face of the man at whom you fired it both before and after you fired it. You could see and hear his agony. You couldn't think of honour and glory with a revolver in your hand, but only of killing and being killed. There was no machine to serve. Life and death were there in your hand in the shape of an elementary arrangement of springs and levers and a few grammes of lead and cordite. He had never handled a revolver in his life before. He examined it carefully. Stamped above the trigger guard was 'Made in U.S.A.' and the name of an American typewriter manufacturer.

This is a characteristic passage of Ambler's prose, from the detached narrative voice to the careful but not overwhelming attention to technical detail (he doesn't tell us the name of the American firm), the almost technical prose, the modulated trace of the American hard-boiled idiom (compare Peter Cheyney's often absurd imitation), and the trope of what we might call existential reduction, the turn from the abstract (internationalism, honour, glory) to the 'elementary.' But it is probably most characteristic in that this is his epitaph for the amateur. Richard Hannay was, you will recall, a mining engineer in Rhodesia before his adventures, but this intrudes on Buchan's plots only in granting him a certain competence and common sense. Winston Graham, the ballistics engineer, has a valuable expertise that thrusts him into the center of an international intrigue but he has little competence or common sense. Thus what is a mere background to Hannay's adventures becomes the center of Graham's – his being a ballistics engineer not only motivates the plot (in that the opponents of the arms sale to Turkey that Graham is arranging want him out of the way) but also provides the source of the hero's coming to self-consciousness.[18]

Thus far, I have written as if all of the Ambler novels were variations on a theme, but though this is in many respects accurate, it is also worthwhile to see the changes from novel to novel. One way of doing this is by following the relation of the shadowy yet omnipresent armaments corporation, Cator & Bliss, through the books, noting not only the lines between it and the villains but also the lines between it and the innocents. The saga of Cator & Bliss begins, as I have said, in *The Dark Frontier* (1936) and it is in that novel that it is most explicit and perhaps least successful. One of the principal villains, Simon Groom, is a director of Cator & Bliss, and the action begins when he tries to hire the physicist Henry Barstow. Barstow refuses, though he is much disconcerted, and after his transformation into Conway Carruthers he does battle with Groom and wins. In *Uncommon Danger* (1937), the journalist Kenton finds himself mixed up in a chase for photographs of documents which would be used in a planned fascist coup in Roumania; in the course of the chase he discovers that the fascists are being aided by Pan-Eurasian Petroleum (who want an oil concession), who turn out to have interlocking ties to Cator & Bliss. In *Cause for Alarm* (1938), Marlow, the engineer, is working for Spartacus Machine Tools in Italy when he gets involved in the sale of armaments information to Vagas, a Nazi spy (who, his dossier tells us, had been an agent for Cator & Bliss). Here Marlow is able to escape and foil the fascist spies by setting Italy and Germany at odds for a while, but an intertextual irony emerges at the very end when Marlow, wanting to be rid of spies and intrigue, accepts a new job as a production engineer – with Cator & Bliss. The story of Winston Graham in *Journey into Fear* (1940) is almost a continuation of Marlow's story, for Graham works directly for Cator & Bliss as a ballistics engineer. The story is set in the midst of the 'phoney war' of early 1940, and for Graham, 'the war meant more work.' Despite Graham's coming to consciousness about his role as something more than technical, and despite the connotations that Cator & Bliss has built up over the earlier novels, in this novel the armaments corporation is no longer really the villain. Despite the 'internationalism' of the arms trade, there is no conflict for Graham between serving the firm, serving the nation, and serving the anti-fascist cause. In a way, the reduction of the plot to the confines of a steamer and its passengers reproduces the reduction of the country house detective story that Ambler had once rejected; the intricate history of post-World War I Europe that is the scene for Dimitrios has been reduced to an existential confrontation between individuals aboard a steamer. One imagines that the Nazi-Soviet pact and the coming of the war had something to do with the sense of constriction in this book. Ambler entered the army in 1940, and wrote screenplays through the 1940s, not returning to the thriller until 1950.

The interest and the power of these tales seems to lie not only in the figurations of fascism and capitalism but also in the figuration of a new class, a new character in the popular imagination, a class of professionals and managers, engineers and technicians. It is a class which is in many ways the hired guns of capital; nevertheless it does work for a wage (if disguised as a salary) and its only capital lies in the certifications of university training. It was this class that was increasingly the readership of these 'serious,' 'literate' thrillers, and indeed Ambler was well suited to be its entertainer; the son of music hall entertainers, he had studied engineering at London University and worked as an advertising copywriter before entering the middle-class music halls – the new thriller and, later, movie screenplays.

These technicians and scientists, often trained at redbrick universities, were breaking from and were held back by the older traditions of the gentleman amateur which held sway at Oxbridge and in the civil service; the public school sporting tradition seemed to cover up simple incompetence in a world where Britain was clearly lagging behind in the second, scientific-technical, industrial revolution. It was a class caught between ideologies of technical efficiency and scientific neutrality and the realities of capitalist work and research practices. And indeed one finds in it some of the same popular front tendencies one finds in Ambler. The young scientists of the 1930s began to organize against the capitalist control of research and science, and the names of J.D. Bernal and J.B.S. Haldane can stand as signs of the influence and importance of left-wing scientists.[19]

If we keep this in mind perhaps we can see why Marlow, in *Cause for Alarm*, tells us that this is not a spy story, that it is not even his own story, but rather the story of Professor Beronelli, late of the University of Bologna. This curious claim in the second paragraph of his tale is almost forgotten by the time the reader meets Beronelli in the penultimate chapter. And even then the story of Professor Beronelli, the great mathematician who has gone mad and thinks he has disproved all of mathematics by proving the possibility of perpetual motion but whose manuscript is nothing but childish scribbles, seems to be one of those stories at which Ambler excels but which are always peripheral to the main story. But there is a sense in which Professor Beronelli's tale

is the one Ambler is always telling, the dark side of Henry
Barstow. Beronelli was driven from the university for his
refusal to work for the fascists; but unlike Barstow, whose
accident transforms him into the heroic Conway Carruthers, Beronelli escapes into his private madness. Between
the magical heroism of Barstow and the mystic madness of
Beronelli walk the innocent technicians and engineers of
Eric Ambler.

Under Western eyes

> Personally I believe questions of ethics are never anything
> but questions of point of view.
>
> — Simon Groom, a director of Cator & Bliss, in Eric Ambler's *The
> Dark Frontier* (1940)

Having given some attention to the story Ambler tells in his
early tales, I want now to turn to the way that story is told.
And this forces us to confront in some way the question of
'point of view.' For though the dominant method of analysis of the novel in Anglo-American literary criticism has
centered on the concept of 'point of view,' on the intricacies
of the relation between the narrator and his or her world
and characters, this tradition seems to have little connection
with the analysis of popular fiction. From the point of view
of literary critics, this is no doubt due to the inadequacy and
lack of complexity of popular fiction; to the analyst of
popular fiction, this seems more due to the limits of the
concept, the way it was developed from a particular Jame-
sian and modernist aesthetic and finds its most interesting
application with those texts. But the case of Ambler, and to
a lesser extent Greene and Maugham, returns this aesthetic
to view, for these are the first thrillers which foreground
questions of point of view. So what I intend to do is not so
much to construct a 'point of view' analysis as to attempt to
explain this foregrounding.

In a way one might expect issues of point of view to be
pre-eminent in the spy novel, for it would seem to lend itself
to spies' obsession with ways of seeing and ways of know-

ing. But it is not really until the novels of Ambler that these concerns emerge as a narrative problem, as the question of how to tell a story or indeed how and whether a certain story can be told. In Ambler's books, there are two related aspects of this question: first, the nature and position of the narrator; and second, the existence of several versions of the same story. Ambler has two basic sorts of narrators. One is the first-person account of the events told by the central participant after the fact. It is the common attempt to reproduce an earlier mode of storytelling, which entailed a shared community and a relatively unmediated communication. The narrator, from a position of experience, tells of an earlier and more innocent self, allowing an occasional present irony, and holding back a past connection for the sake of suspense, for the sake of the story. Ambler's place in this tradition might be marked by placing his Marlow (of *Cause for Alarm*) between Conrad's Marlow and Chandler's Marlowe. Conrad's Marlow tells his tales to listeners figured in the book itself; his detachment, irony, and lucidity fit well the picture Sartre drew of this variety of nineteenth-century bourgeois storytelling:

> the adventure was a brief disturbance and is over with. It was told from the viewpoint of experience and wisdom; it is listened to from the viewpoint of order ... everything concurs in symbolizing the stable bourgeoisie of the end of the century which thinks that nothing more will happen and which believes in the eternity of capitalist organization.

Ambler's Marlow shares some of these traits though there is no evening gathering of men who listen to the story and the tone of his opening is surely more frantic. He is apologetic: 'I am perfectly aware that, even though I am telling the story, I do not cut a very heroic figure in it; and no man likes to be reminded that he is a nitwit'; and he is much less detached, the events having concluded just before the telling, in 'this year, 1937.' Nevertheless, the story is told from the point of view of order, and just as Conrad's Marlow sets out to tell the tragedy of Kurtz, so Ambler's Marlow means to tell us the tragedy of Beronelli. We see here, as we did with the rhetoric of civilization and the jungle, the plots of Empire rearticulated as the plots of anti-fascism.[20]

But there is also a touch of Chandler's Marlowe in Ambler, the protagonist's narrative which is not told after the fact but during the event, thus giving the reader not a balanced and measured tale but a series of incidents whose internal coherence is never entirely clear. One can see how this could well serve the Ambler story of the bumbling innocent and it is curious that he uses it so rarely. The second half of *The Dark Frontier*, narrated by the American journalist Casey, is a somewhat awkward version; it is not until Ambler's later fine stories about the mercenary Arthur Abdul Simpson (*The Light of Day*, 1962, and *Dirty Story*, 1967) that he successfully adapts the hard-boiled conventions to his own purposes (something he shares with Len Deighton, whose own successful adaptation of the hard-boiled, *The Ipcress File*, was published in 1962).[21]

The other main narrator of the Ambler tale is the omniscient even olympian historian who narrates *The Mask of Dimitrios* and *Uncommon Danger*. This cynical, detached narrator with his sometimes labored ironies and occasionally pretentious historical meditations is a mark of the Ambler metaphysic, the meshing of the formal and the ideological point of view. This historian sets the tale of Dimitrios against a matter-of-fact narrative of European history since the Great War; but he also delights in the role of chance and contingency, and in the grotesque, indeed melodramatic, confusion of levels that it causes.

In an age which no longer believes in Providence, this historian tells us, chance takes its place, and the occasional artistry that can be seen in the workings of chance is really nothing more than the grotesque. Thus the narrator gives us, in *Uncommon Danger*, a detailed family history of Achilles Karl Hoesch in order to account for his unusual name, which, when combined with the accident of his being shot in the heel, makes a grotesque newspaper headline – ACHILLES' HEEL – out of an unnewsworthy story and thus involves him in the narrator's plot of spies, a plot on which the fate of Eastern Europe hangs. Indeed, as this historian says, 'the situation in which a person, imagining fondly that he is in charge of his own destiny, is, in fact, the sport of circumstances beyond his control, is always fascinating.'[22]

However, both of these types of narrators – the actor telling his own tale after the event, and the cynical historian showing us the ironic twistings of those who think they are more than puppets – are thrown into question by the other aspect of the foregrounding of point of view, the impossibility of reconciling into either of those supposedly authoritative voices the many stories told about the same event by different actors and observers. The classic version is Latimer's attempt to bring together all of the testimonies about Dimitrios into a 'biography,' an enterprise that is mocked by the narrator. But even the narrator is only able to trace Latimer's steps, noting the ironies, but is unable to tell the story of Dimitrios himself. In most mysteries, the 'hermeneutic code,' Roland Barthes's term for the aspect of the narrative that poses and attempts to solve an enigma and expresses the narrative's search for truth, is worked through the clues collected and judged by a detective figure; in *The Mask of Dimitrios*, the 'detective,' Latimer, is merely a pretext for the telling of a variety of tales from different points of view, none of which reveal the 'truth' about Dimitrios.[23]

At this point we must ask why we find this foregrounding of point of view, why the questions of the ambiguity and insolubility of the plot emerge in a popular genre, one which we don't usually assume to be overly concerned with epistemological questions. One reason has to do with the new and growing reading public for the Ambler thriller, the shift from what in the rhetoric of the 1930s was called a 'lowbrow' public to a 'middlebrow' public. But this 'literariness' that marks the middlebrow novels in the form of a heightening of issues of point of view is also an ideological move. And here I would reverse Simon Groom's comment that questions of ethics are questions of point of view, and argue that the centrality of point of view marks the dominance of an ethical mode of thought. The concern for the ambiguity of all points of view, the obsessive story of the loss of innocence, and the demystifying reduction of all civilization to violence and brute force: all these aspects of the Ambler metaphysic join to form a concern for individual ethical decisions in the context of certain established and perman-ent aspects of human nature and experience. This is what licenses an interpretation like Ralph Harper's *The World of the Thriller*, a reading of the thriller, particularly the novels of Ambler, through the categories of existentialism, as a literature of crisis and boundary situations: 'in the end, the thriller, each novel, must be rated according to whether its heroes stand firm in the middle of chaos, or whether they are converted by chaos and are damned.'[24] Indeed, such an interpretation is based on the manifest rhetoric and ex-planation systems of the Ambler novels: one half of it can be seen in the speech by the journalist Kenton quoted above (p. 72) which speaks of the ethical rather than political basis for his decision to resist violence and not to com-promise. Complementing this focus on individual choice is the sense of the chaos and absurdity of history which marks the comments of the various narrators on the role of chance and coincidence in history.

However, to explain this ethical and existentialist ex-planation system at work in the world of the Ambler thriller in terms of an existential philosophy and vocabulary, as Harper does, is not sufficient and does not come to terms with the historical character of that very philosophy and vocabulary. Rather I think that we need to explain it in terms of the plots that resist representation; the difficulty of telling the story has to do not with the difficulties of all storytelling but with the difficulties of representing these particular stories. For what Ambler gets from Conrad's spy stories is not only the concern for narrative point of view and the existential metaphysic of civilization and chaos but also the strategy of placing the East, and particularly the revolutionary activity of the East, 'under Western eyes.' The English language teacher who admits his inability to com-prehend the Russian revolutionaries in *Under Western Eyes* is a precursor of Ambler's innocent Englishmen abroad. So it is worth looking at the representation of revolution in the 'serious' or 'existential' thriller.

To do this, we can turn briefly back to W. Somerset Maugham's *Ashenden* (1928), the first of these thrillers. *Ashenden* was first published as a novel, though its incidents are tied together only by the character of Ashenden, and in later editions Maugham repackaged it as a collection of short stories. The ambiguity is interesting insofar as it is a symptom of the failure of any unifying plot. Ashenden, a well-known writer recruited into the secret service during the Great War, is involved in a series of discrete episodes in Switzerland where he is stationed:

> it must be confessed that for the small fry like himself to be a member of the secret service was not as adventurous an affair as the public thought. Ashenden's official existence was as orderly and monotonous as a city clerk's. He saw his spies at stated intervals and paid them their wages; when he could get hold of a new one he engaged him, gave him his instructions and sent him off to Germany; he waited for the information that came through and dispatched it . . .

As a result, the lack of a unified plot in *Ashenden* is reproduced in Ashenden's own existence:

> Being no more than a tiny rivet in a vast and complicated machine, he never had the advantage of seeing a completed action . . . It was as unsatisfactory as one of those modern novels that give you a number of unrelated episodes and expect you by piecing them together to construct in your mind a connected narrative.

The unrelated episodes that Maugham gives us are exemplary tales of innocents mistaken for spies and other innocents destroyed as pawns in a larger game. It is the repeated oscillation between the protestation that 'Damn it all, we are gentlemen' and don't play the game that way, and the actual playing out of the game in the most sordid and calculating way.[25]

However, if there is a climax to this disconnected

narrative, it comes when Ashenden is sent to Russia for 'his most important mission.' This is loosely based on Maugham's own experience which he notes in the preface to *Ashenden*:

> In 1917 I went to Russia. I was sent to prevent the Bolshevik revolution and to keep Russia in the war. The reader will know that my efforts did not meet with success.

So too the reader knows that Ashenden's efforts are doomed from the first moment: 'though he had been set to do something that was beyond human possibility he did not know this and was prepared to set upon his task with confidence.' What follows are an account of an old love affair with a Russian woman, sparked by meeting her again, and an account of the 'tragedy' of the 'highbrow' and talkative American businessman Mr. Harrington, whose acquaintance Ashenden makes on the train across Russia and continues in a Petrograd hotel. As the Provisional Government falls and the Bolsheviks take power, Mr. Harrington concludes his business deals: 'History was in the making and Mr. Harrington minded his own business.' On the morning after the taking of the Winter Palace, a distressed Mr. Harrington wonders why there are no servants in the hotel, and why his laundry has not been returned to him. He refuses to leave and goes off in search of his washing. He is later found dead, clutching his washing.[26]

The story of Mr. Harrington, comic in his self-assured blindness to history, is a foil against which the 'Western eyes' of Ashenden are defined. But it is also the only story those Western eyes can relate. Ashenden fails not only to prevent the revolution but also to represent it. His distance from the revolution is figured in his decision years earlier to give up his romance with Anastasia, a romance too much 'like a Russian novel . . . all very dreadful and wonderful and shattering.'[27]

Continental revolutions also figure in the entertainments of Graham Greene, from the failed attempt of Dr. Czinner to return to Belgrade to join an uprising in *Stamboul Train*

(1932), to the mixed success of D., a medieval scholar who has chosen to work as an agent for the Spanish republicans, in his attempt to buy coal in England for the republicans in *The Confidential Agent* (1939). In both cases the central issues of the novel have to do less with representing revolutionary struggle than with the choice by an intellectual to serve that struggle, thus highlighting issues of point of view and dilemmas of faith and ethics (we will see later how this is worked out in detail in Greene's *The Human Factor*).

The difficulty of representing revolution in the East haunts Ambler's thrillers as well. Indeed, his first novel, *The Dark Frontier*, finds its climax in the successful peasant revolution in Ixania; and, as befits this extravagant romance, the hero Barstow/Carruthers both makes contact with the revolutionaries and is central to their success. Nevertheless, the actual representation of the revolution happens elsewhere, and we see only the exploits of Carruthers; the narrator, the American journalist Casey, tells us (as if he were John Reed): 'I have written elsewhere and at length on the subject of the Ixanian revolution, of the political situation that led up to it and of the dramatic twenty-four hours in which the peasants' *coup d'état* was effected.'[28]

In the later novels, the representation of revolution recedes as ironic points of view and conflicting stories come to the fore. In *The Mask of Dimitrios*, the struggles in Eastern Europe are viewed through Western eyes as Latimer tries to fathom the meaning of the life of Dimitrios. Revolutionary activity comes to be figured in particular characters rather than particular events or movements. Thus, in *Epitaph for a Spy*, one of the hotel guests Vadassy thinks is a Nazi spy turns out to be a German Communist who had spent two years in a concentration camp and is hiding from the Gestapo under an assumed name. So in the midst of this thriller we get an interlude as Schimler tells Vadassy his life story; and, at the end, as the innocent Vadassy is cleared of suspicion, he learns that his new friend has been captured and returned to Germany.

But the crucial figures who turn up in both *Uncommon*

Danger and *Cause for Alarm* are the good-natured Soviet spies Andreas Zaleshoff and his sister Tamara, who help the English innocents out of the tangled web into which they have fallen. Zaleshoff has his own purposes which often further entangle the Englishman, but all works out in the end. Zaleshoff educates the Englishman with witty parables of European politics and helps in negotiating the new experience of danger and violence; as Marlow concludes at the end of *Cause for Alarm*, 'you could not help liking Zaleshoff.'[29]

In a formal sense Zaleshoff serves as what Vladimir Propp, in his account of the structure of folktales, called a 'donor,' that crucial function that gives the hero the means to accomplish its goal or win its contest. In an elaboration of Propp's notion, Fredric Jameson has noted that

> the donor is the element which explains the change described in the story, that which supplies a sufficiently asymmetrical force to make it interesting to tell, and which is therefore somehow responsible for the 'storiness' of the story . . . The basic interpersonal and dramatic relationship of the narrative tale is therefore neither the head-on direct one of love nor that of hatred and conflict, but rather this lateral relationship of the hero to the ex-centric figure of the donor.[30]

And indeed the center of these stories is the relationship of the Englishman (Kenton and Marlow) and the Soviet spy Zaleshoff. Let me further suggest that this figure of the union of the English scientist or technician and the Soviet spy, a union that Ambler narrates as a happy story, becomes a central trope in the popular imagination and continues to resonate in thrillers as well as in the celebrated cases of the atom bomb spies Fuchs and Nunn May, and of Kim Philby. Indeed, one direction that the Ambler thriller can take is exemplified by the little-known but interesting tale of Cold War 1955 by Robert Harling, *The Enormous Shadow*, where a journalist discovers that a young Labour MP and a distinguished mathematician are spying for the Soviets. The mathematician's wife says of him: 'Yes I suppose in a way he was a Communist. He was never a member of the party, but politically they had his sympathies. It's not unusual with scientists and technicians with his background, is it?'[31] In 1955 this metaphoric juxtaposition – British scientist/ Soviet spy – has become a 'villain,' and though Harling deftly paints its complexities, we have returned to the world of Conrad: in most thrillers, as in popular discourse, radicalism was seen in the 1950s, as E.P. Thompson writes, 'as projections of the neuroses of maladjusted intellectuals' and that 'theme entered the repertoire of Hollywood spy dramas.'[32]Even for Ambler the figure of socialist refugee or Soviet spy as 'donor' to the British technician 'hero' became untenable in a serious way, marked as it was by the Stalinism of the Popular Front. In the last of his early thrillers, *Journey into Fear*, where, as we saw earlier, there is a more benign version of the armaments corporation, we also see a farcical version of Schimler and Zaleshoff in Mathis, a 'hen-pecked' French factory manager who is a socialist and whom Graham meets on the steamer. For all his good nature, he is no guide to the 'real' world like Zaleshoff; rather he is innocent of the deadly struggles going on around him. The union between Graham and Mathis takes the form of a joke, intended only to annoy Mathis's respectable wife: Mathis's imaginary 'plot to blow up the Bank of France, seize the Chamber of Deputies, shoot the two hundred families, and set up a Communist government.'[33] The later Ambler gives up even this; his protagonists, particularly Arthur Abdul Simpson, are the hired guns themselves, the mercenaries out for personal survival.

If it is the historical consequences of the Soviet revolution of 1917 that are directly invoked in these various attempts to represent the East under the Western eyes of Maugham, Greene, and Ambler, and in its condensation in the contradictory and unstable figure of the union of the English scientist and the Soviet spy, there was a situation closer to home, unmentioned, even repressed, that produced these thrillers. For the first Communist spy panic was the Zinoviev letter of 1924 with its supposed orders from Moscow to British workers. Perhaps the story so difficult to narrate was not only that of a revolution in the East which seemed incomprehensible to Western eyes, but that of the defeated and repressed General Strike of 1926. The General Strike does not directly appear in the thriller, but its imaginative impact may be gauged by Graham Greene's account in his autobiography; he tells of becoming a special constable patrolling 'a beautiful hushed London that we were not to know again until the blitz':

> there was the exciting sense of living on a frontier, close to violence . . . A few years later my sympathies would have lain with them [the strikers], but the great depression was still some years away: the middle class had not yet been educated by the hunger marchers. On the side of the Establishment it was a game, a break in the monotony of earning a secure living, at its most violent the atmosphere was that of a rugger match played against a team from a rather rough council school which didn't stick to the conventional rules.[34]

Greene's two figures – the sense of the General Strike as a frontier between a threatening, violent reality and the political 'innocence' of the English middle classes, and the metaphor of the General Strike as a game no longer played by the rules – are the cover stories that dominate the thriller after 1926, cover stories of the General Strike and of the transition from the heroic world of Buchan to the ambiguities of Maugham, Greene, and Ambler.

4
Licensed to look

Thrillers of the spectacle

With James Bond, the spy thriller enters its moment of greatest popularity. Whereas earlier we found espionage themes coming to dominate the thriller generally, we now see the espionage thriller coming to dominate the entire field of popular fiction. Tales of spies are no longer one part of popular culture; they are at its center. James Bond transcended the novels and films which brought him to life, and joined that small group of fictional characters who are known by many who never read or saw the 'original' texts – figures like Robinson Crusoe and Sherlock Holmes. But this presence of Bond in the popular imagination is itself only one part of the presence of espionage in the culture of the late 1950s and early 1960s: spy stories proliferated in novels, on film and on TV; in the daily newspapers, the sensational cases of George Blake and Kim Philby marked the spy fever of the 1960s. Christopher Booker, in a history of the period's culture, writes:

> The curious way in which the Bond phenomenon had become a shadow to the history of the age, had been given a further twist in March 1961 when an American magazine had revealed that one of the most fervent Bond readers was President Kennedy. Partly aided by

this revelation, in 1961 and 1962, the sales of Bond books on both sides of the Atlantic had soared. Now, by the end of 1962, with the arrival of new authors such as Len Deighton (north London) and John le Carré (Oxford early 50s), a Foreign Office official, 'spy literature', like satire, seemed to be turning into an industry. It was also in November 1962, that with the arrival of James Bond on the screen, played by the former Carnaby Street model and Royal Court actor Sean Connery (Glasgow), the record-breaking *Dr. No* marked the beginning of a turn in British cinema away from 'Northern Realism' and indeed 'naturalism' of any kind towards an altogether more colourful and sensational kind of fantasy. The real explanation for this new popularity of spy stories, in fact, was not so much that they were a reflection of the increase in real life spying, as a more subtle reflection of the *Zeitgeist*.[1]

Though the *Zeitgeist* is easier to invoke than to define, the spy novel is in a sense the war novel of the Cold War, the cover story of an era of decolonization and, particularly after the débâcle at Suez in 1956, the definitive loss of Britain's role as a world power. This flowering of the spy thriller will be the subject of the next two chapters, the first on Ian Fleming's James Bond tales, and the second on the quite different spy novels that emerged from the same moment – the tales of looking-glass wars written by John le Carré, Graham Greene, Len Deighton, and others.

Ian Fleming's first novel about James Bond, *Casino Royale*, was published in 1953; twelve more novels and the two collections of short stories were published by 1965. But the moment of Bond does not really begin until the publication of *Casino Royale* in Pan paperback in 1956, and the serialization of *From Russia, With Love* in the *Daily Express* in 1957; after which the sales of the Bond books took off, reaching a peak in 1964 and 1965 in the wake of the release of the first Bond films. For it was the Bond books that brought the American paperback revolution to Britain. 'They were,' John Sutherland writes, 'a breakthrough comparable in some ways to Lane's, thirty years earlier,' that is, to Allen Lane's Penguins. Pan claimed that ten of the first eighteen million-sellers in Britain were Bond novels.[2]

And just as this qualitative leap in the mode of production of popular fiction must be marked off from the fiction that preceded it, so there is also a discontinuity between the spy thrillers of the first half of the century and this new expansion of the thriller – a discontinuity that ought not be effaced by the conventions of literary histories of the genre. For no formal account of the genre's progress explains the Bond books and their enormous popularity. Surely the logic of increasing verisimilitude, the sense that each new breakthrough in the spy novel marks a more convincing code of realism, does not account for Fleming's fantastic tales, despite his skill at using the reality-effect in details, a skill that led Kingsley Amis to define that device as the 'Fleming effect.'[3] Rather what is remarkable is the way that the earlier spy thriller had spent much of its force; both Greene and Ambler had largely given up the spy thriller by the late 1940s, and they were to return to the genre in the 1960s because of the new centrality accorded it by the work of Fleming, le Carré, and Deighton.

So how are we to account for this new thriller, and how describe its constituents? The obvious place to begin would be with the figure of James Bond himself, particularly in light of the way that he managed to transcend his textual embodiment and join Sherlock Holmes as a major character in the popular imagination. The difficulty lies in the variety of James Bonds there are. Some critics find him essentially a continuation of the tradition of snobbery with violence, an all too familiar aristocratic clubman with an even greater degree of sadism thrown in. Others see him as a modern and modernizing hero, the 'perfect pipe-dream figure for organization man,' as Julian Symons put it.[4] Some see him as a 'cold warrior,' a racist and a sexist; others stress the moments when he seems to parody these. Is he really an amateur out defending the realm, an updated Richard Hannay (after all, Hannay's amateur status did not preclude his working for the government), or is he the consummate professional, totally subordinate to the service? Is his amateurism maintained by his game-like attitude toward his missions and his sense of improvisation, or does his training and competence together with his lack of developed self-consciousness put him firmly in the camp of the professional, doing a job? Or, to put it another way, is he really an upper-class clubman, trained in the public school ethic, or is he an Americanized 'classless' modernizer, bringing 'the white heat of technology' to the spy thriller? Is he a superhero, or is he, as Ian Fleming thought, absolutely ordinary?

No doubt readers will answer these questions in part through their sense of the character, their after-image of the tales, and in part by citing pieces of evidence, kernels of character, the attributes mentioned in one place or another that build the narrative illusion which is 'a character.' So an Amis will point out that Bond is not really an aristocrat because he never drinks port or sherry. The point is that each set of attributes can be countered with another; Bond is a contested figure who has been accented in a number of ways. Indeed, the story of the casting for the film Bond illustrates this well: Fleming himself preferred David Niven, a figure who had played upper-class characters. However, after the choice of Sean Connery, Fleming remarked, 'Not quite the idea I had of Bond, but he would be if I wrote the books over again.'[5] Connery was meant to give more of a 'man of the people' image to Bond, and Christopher Booker argues that Connery's Bond was part of a 'new class' of image producers that dominated the culture of the late 1950s and early 1960s, mixing lower-class origins with media affluence and consumerism. The later casting of Roger Moore as Bond returned the character to an older, more class-ridden paradigm since Moore was strongly identified with his television portrayal of the gentleman outlaw of the 1930s, the Saint.

But the contest over Bond's public image was already a part of the novels. In *From Russia, With Love,* the 1957 tale which I will examine in some detail in this chapter, the point of the Russian plot is to kill Bond 'WITH IGNOMINY'.

They wish to humiliate and destroy not only the man but the image, the myth which is important to the British secret service. The strength of the British, we are told, 'lies in the myth – the myth of Scotland Yard, of Sherlock Holmes, of the Secret Service . . . this myth is a hindrance which it would be good to set aside . . . Have they no one who is a hero to the organization? Someone who is admired and whose ignominious destruction would cause dismay? Myths are built on heroic deeds and heroic people. Have they no such men? . . . ' The answer, of course, is: 'There is a man called Bond.'[6]

The plot to destroy Bond's image itself employs that image: the Russians convince the British secret service that one of their women agents has fallen in love with a photograph of Bond. The manifest absurdity of this plot is explained away by Bond's superior, M., who invokes a 'common' behaviour in a society of images: 'Suppose you happened to be a film star instead of being in this particular trade. You'd get daft letters from girls all over the world stuffed with Heaven knows what sort of rot about not being able to live without you and so on. Here's a silly girl doing a secretary's job in Moscow . . . And she gets what I believe they call a "crush" on this picture [of Bond], just as secretaries all over the world get crushes on these dreadful faces in the magazines.' Therefore Bond's job is to behave like the image: 'It is with an image she has fallen in love. Behave like that image.'[7]

In a way, our relation to Bond as readers is not far removed from that of Tatiana Romanova, investing our own energies in a mere image. This has two different effects. First, and less significantly, it means that Bond is something of a cipher which can be invested with a variety of content. But, more importantly, these different investments do not seem to distort an original Bond, for the effect of the Bond image is to efface its origins. Bond is a character of the present, not one with a particular class history, or regional rootedness. He is not a type, and we feel the self-mocking humor when, at one point in *The Man With the Golden Gun*, Bond claims that 'EYE AM A SCOTTISH PEASANT AND

EYE WILL ALWAYS FEEL AT HOME BEING A SCOTTISH
PEASANT.'[8]

Here we do find his link with that new class that Booker
speaks of: though they are not so much a class as themselves
avatars of a particular image of affluence, fashion, modern-
ity, and classlessness. These 'New Aristocrats' were creators
of images: Booker cites pop singers (the Beatles, Mick
Jagger), photographers (David Bailey), interior decorators,
spy novelists (Deighton), actors (Michael Caine, Connery),
and fashion designers. Though they may have come from
working-class, lower-middle-class and northern backgrounds, the effect of the aristocracy of images was to efface
their origins: the jacket notes on Len Deighton's novels
which variously claim that he is the son of a chauffeur or the
son of the Governor General of the Windward Islands,
which have him educated at either the Royal College of Art
or at Eton and Oxford, and which attribute to him a variety
of jobs, are a playful example of this effacement and
confusion of origins.

Nevertheless, the analogy between Bond as image and the
brief reign of the 'New Aristocrats' is merely the beginning
of an explanation of the cultural meaning and power of
Bond: what it does is point us to the crucial term, the
production and proliferation of images. In what follows I
will look at the way two central aspects of the thriller, the
game and the Empire, are reconstructed in the tales of
Fleming in the terms of a society of the spectacle, and will
then look at the meaning of the new prominence of the
codes of sexuality in the Fleming thriller.

Killing time

In *The Spy Who Loved Me*, James Bond tries to explain the
enterprise of spying to Vivienne Michel:

> It's nothing but a complicated game, really. But then
> so's international politics, diplomacy – all the trap-
> pings of nationalism and the power complex that goes
> on between countries. Nobody will stop playing the
> game. It's like the hunting instinct.[9]

In many ways this is, as we have seen, the oldest trope in the book. The figure of the Great Game for spying and international intrigue comes in a heroic version in the early thrillers of Buchan and Sapper, but it is no less present when it is unveiled as a mystification in the cynical tales of Ambler and Maugham. In Fleming, we find a new inflection: it is still a heroic and necessary game and one that Bond enjoys playing; nevertheless, it is clearly a deadly serious game, one for professionals not amateurs.

But much as the Bond thrillers draw on these older paradigms of the game and the ethic of sportsmanship and fair play, reworking them and at times parodying them, the game also takes on a new significance through the foregrounding of two sorts of game: first, the way the plot structure itself resembles a game, and second, the attention to the representation of a variety of games in the books.

The game-like nature of the Bond tales was the subject of Umberto Eco's important and influential essay on narrative structure in Fleming's novels. He argued that the novels were structured like a game with a set of rules, pieces, and conventional moves: the reader knows the rules, the pieces, and the moves – even the outcome is not a surprise – and watches the game unfold. The sequence of moves is strictly determined with only the slightest variation. And not only is the story constructed like a game but the story itself is a game, a contest, a series of what Eco calls 'play situations.'[10]

This game-like nature of the tales, which Bond himself recognizes in his oft-repeated comment about his 'playing Red Indians,' also makes for the formalism of the books (and indeed licenses the formalism of Eco's analysis). All existential or psychological elements are carefully excluded, as we can see if we think of neighboring genres. The tradition of the thriller as a hunt, for example, which the Bond books resemble, usually takes the extremity of men hunting men as an example of an existential confrontation with the primitive, the instinctual, and so forth. In Geoffrey Household's *Rogue Male* (1939), for example, we see the reduction of all life to a 'kill or be killed' situation, as the hunter-hunted narrator progressively sheds all trappings of civilization. One can see a similar process in more recent hunt tales such as Desmond Bagley's *Running Blind* (1970) or Gavin Lyall's *The Most Dangerous Game* (1964) (where the most dangerous game – in the sense of prey – is men). Bond's adventures, though similar, do not evoke this. They are, first of all, of a serial nature; far from being the exceptional reduction of civilized man to his 'true' primitive nature, his adventures are all part of the job. They are closer to that other popular formula, 'capers,' which are elaborately and professionally planned operations, the accomplishment of a particularly difficult coup, as in the assassination of de Gaulle in Frederick Forsyth's *The Day of the Jackal* (1971) or the *coup d'état* in his *The Dogs of War* (1974). There is little mystery involved in these adventures: suspense reigns. Rather than the continually deferred question of whodunit, we have the continually repeated question of what happened next or even the technical question of how was it accomplished.

If this begins to explain the absence of an existential explanatory system, we can see the lack of real psychological motivation by comparing Bond to the formula of the avenger, exploited in a paradigmatic way in the stories of Mickey Spillane, stories which are often linked to those of Fleming and which had a significant influence on Fleming. By exploiting the desire for revenge, Spillane produces books which are fully as formulaic as the Bond tales but which are by no means game-like.

This game-like structure comes to a sort of narrative self-consciousness in *From Russia, With Love*. In *From Russia, With Love*, Bond's Turkish ally, Kerim, tells Bond: 'But I was not brought up to "be a sport" . . . This is not a game to me. It is a business. For you it is different. You are a gambler.' Like the Hairless Mexican in Maugham's *Ashenden*, Kerim 'hasn't had the advantages of a public-school education.' But it is his metaphor that marks the limit of the text:

This is a billiard table. An easy, flat, green billiard table. And you have hit your white ball and it is travelling easily and quietly towards the red. The pocket is alongside. Fatally, inevitably, you are going to hit the red and the red is going into that pocket. It is the law of the billiard table, the law of the billiard room. But, outside the orbit of these things, a jet pilot has fainted and his plane is diving straight at that billiard room, or a gas main is about to explode, or lightning is about to strike. And the building collapses on top of you and on top of the billiard table. Then what has happened to that white ball that could not miss the red ball, and to the red ball that could not miss the pocket? The white ball could not miss according to the laws of the billiard table. But the laws of the billiard table are not the only laws, and the laws governing the progress of this train, and of you to your destiny, are also not the only laws in this particular game.[11]

Indeed, this sense of different levels of rules is more pronounced in *From Russia, With Love* than in most Fleming tales. Here we find a less pronounced version of the formula found in the other books: there is no game between Bond and the villain, no fantastic plot for world domination by the villain. Both the original plot – to destroy not so much Bond as the image of Bond – and the final struggle with Red Grant in the curious 'battle of the books' (which we will examine in the next chapter) show a self-consciousness about the laws of Fleming's own 'billiard table.' And the ending, the quite unexpected and unrelieved death of Bond, seems to be a stepping outside of those laws. Ironically, perhaps, though *From Russia, With Love* killed off Bond, it surely didn't kill off his image: the peak of Bond's celebrity began with the serialization of *From Russia, With Love* in the *Daily Express*. So Fleming dutifully resurrected Bond at the beginning of the next novel, *Dr. No*, setting him up for new games.

However, the appearance of the game in the narrative structure is not the only aspect of the game figure that is new in the Fleming tales. So too is the extraordinary amount of space devoted to representing games and sports. One of

Fleming's talents is as a sportswriter, whether he is writing about Bond's golf match with Goldfinger, the baccarat game against Le Chiffre, the bridge game against Drax, or the ski chase in *On Her Majesty's Secret Service*. In part, these are used to play out the conventions of the ethic of sportsmanship. In *Moonraker*, for example, Sir Hugo Drax is introduced as a quite extraordinary man – with one reservation: he cheats at cards. As M. says, 'don't forget that cheating at cards can still smash a man. In so-called Society, it's about the only crime that can still finish you, whoever you are.' Nevertheless, Bond's victory over Drax, and over Goldfinger, who cheats at golf, comes not through revealing the cheater to Society, the arbiter, but through cheating in return. After all, as Bond thinks in the course of his deception of Goldfinger, 'there was more to this than a game of golf. It was Bond's duty to win.'[12]

A second use of the games is to establish a system of national characters. National characters are in part delineated by the sorts of games that are played. So the Russians are chess players: Kronsteen in *From Russia, With Love*, the 'Wizard of Ice,' is a chess master and spymaster who sees people as pawns and recalls cases as he does gambits. Bond and the British, on the other hand, are gamblers, both in the casino and in the field.

But the representation of games and sports has less to do with either the older public school ethic or the stereotypes of national character than with the new ethic of consumption and leisure. For the games Bond plays, like the liquor he drinks and the automobiles he drives, serve as a kind of guide to leisure. The sports represented are not the public school cricket pitch, nor the aristocratic blood sports and yachting, nor the working-class spectator sport of football: they are the consumer sports of golf, skiing, and casino gambling. They have the glamor of being the sports of the wealthy, the sports of the holiday on the Continent, yet are relatively free from traditional class connotations. Like Bond's vodka martinis, they are neither port nor a pint at the pub.

But though these books are themselves for killing time,

they are not simply guides to consumption, 'how-to' books, rehearsals for leisure. Rather they are also redemptions of consumption, an investing of the trivial contests of the fairway with global intrigue. If, in *Goldfinger*, Fleming devotes three times as much space to the golf match as to the robbery of Fort Knox, this is surely because the detail and attention to the contest the reader can imagine not only prepares him or her for the absurdity of the Fort Knox plot, but is also a more interesting story than the Fort Knox plot. For just as the spy stories of le Carré tell tales of white-collar work, so Fleming's adventures are really tales of leisure, tales where leisure is not a packaged, commodified 'holiday,' filling up a space of 'time off' from work, an acceptable moment to 'kill time,' but is an adventure, a meaningful time, a time of life and death – in the words of *From Russia, With Love*, a killing time.

Thrilling cities

All my life I have been interested in adventure and, abroad, I have enjoyed the *frisson* of leaving the wide, well-lit streets and venturing up back alleys in search of the hidden, authentic pulse of towns. It was perhaps this habit that turned me into a writer of thrillers, and by the time I made the two journeys that produced these essays, I had certainly got into the way of looking at people and places and things through a thriller-writer's eye.

– Ian Fleming, *Thrilling Cities* (1964)

In his essay on James Bond, Tony Bennett examines the narrative codes that structure the stories and argues

that the ideologies of sexism and imperialism are inscribed within the very form of the Bond novels . . . As the relations between Bond and the villain and between Bond and the girl develop and move toward their resolution, a series of collateral ideological tensions is thus simultaneously worked through and resolved. It is in this way that the Bond novels achieve

their 'ideological effect' – the effect, figuratively
speaking, of placing women back in position beneath
men and putting England back on top.[13]

His account of the relation between ideologies and narrative codes is, I think, a persuasive and productive one; and
his focus on the 'imperialist code' and the 'sexist code' is
well taken: these are surely codes that unite larger ideological themes with the detail of the narratives of Fleming.
However, the very names he gives these codes seems to elide
the specificity of Fleming's reconstruction of ideologies of
Empire and the novelty of his construction of an ideology of
sexuality. So rather than seeing the tales as a modernized
version of the imperialist adventure tale, it seems to me that
their clearly imperialist and racist ideologies are constructed through a narrative code of tourism; and rather
than seeing the sexual codes as a 'sexist code,' the reposi-
tioning of the 'girl,' who is 'out-of-place sexually,' in the
traditional ordering of sexual difference, one can see that
the 'girl' is put into place in a new ordering of the sex/gender
system, through the narrative code of pornography. In both
cases, I will argue in the following two sections, Bond's
'licence to kill' is less significant than his 'licence to look.'

Travel and tourism make up much of the interest and
action of a Bond thriller. The final and climactic quarter of
From Russia, With Love takes place on the fabled Orient
Express; the final struggle with Goldfinger occurs aboard a
BOAC airliner; and in almost all the novels some space is
given to narrating Bond's travels by plane and train. Umberto Eco argues that the 'Journey' is one of the principal
'play situations' in the novel. And indeed, the representation
of traveling also works in capturing the reader, a reader who
is often traveling himself or herself. From the W.H. Smiths
at the nineteenth-century railway station to those at the
twentieth-century airport, the sale and consumption of
cheap fiction has been tied to the means of transport. Bond
himself exemplifies this as he reads a copy of Eric Ambler's
The Mask of Dimitrios on the flight into Istanbul in *From
Russia, With Love* and when he picks up the 'latest

Raymond Chandler' for his flight in *Goldfinger*.

Furthermore, the stories have a relation to tourism in that almost all of them take place in exotic locales. Only one Bond novel, *Moonraker*, takes place primarily in Britain, in striking contrast to the clubland thrillers of Buchan, Sapper, Dornford Yates, and Leslie Charteris. In part, this is a consequence of the post-war fiction market, which, as John Sutherland has remarked, was oriented to international Anglophone sales and encouraged international settings in writers as unalike as Fleming and Graham Greene. The loss of British world economic and political hegemony was accompanied by the loss of a cultural centrality; the obverse of imaginary centrality to the world of the British agent Bond is the marginality of Britain as a place of adventure.

But tourism takes its place as a central narrative code in the Fleming novels in a deeper way by infiltrating Fleming's prose and organizing the Fleming 'world system.' For the prose of the travel book and the tour guide is present in Fleming's work far beyond his own travel book, *Thrilling Cities*. In some cases, as in *Live and Let Die*, tourist guides supplant Fleming's prose entirely as the reader is treated to several pages about Haitian voodoo lifted directly from Patrick Leigh Fermor's *The Travellers Tree*; a footnote tells us that this is 'one of the great travel books.' In other cases, as in *You Only Live Twice*, there are tedious sections of straightforward travelogue by Fleming, filling up a sketchy plot with what one chapter title aptly terms 'Instant Japan.' But even in less extreme cases, the prose of the tourist guide inflects much of these novels, often lending them their interest and a certain degree of verisimilitude. So in *From Russia, With Love* we often find passages like this one of Bond awakening in Istanbul:

> Bond got out of bed, drew back the heavy plush red curtains and leant on the iron balustrade and looked out over one of the most famous views in the world – on his right the still waters of the Golden Horn, on his left the dancing waves of the unsheltered Bosphorus, and, in between, the tumbling roofs, soaring minarets

and crouching mosques of Pera. After all, his choice had been good. The view made up for many bedbugs and much discomfort.[14]

Here we find an epitome of the tourist's experience: the moment of relaxed visual contemplation from above, leaning on the balustrade; the aesthetic reduction of a social entity, the city, to a natural object, coterminous with the waves of the sea; the calculations of the tourist's economy, exchanging physical discomfort for a more 'authentic' view; and the satisfaction at having made the right exchange, having 'got' the experience, possessed the 'view.' Indeed, if we see Fleming's travel writing, like his sports writing, as the presence of the discourse of the spectacle, the discourse of consumer society, we can see how its effect is to redeem these activities of consumption, to heroize them. For the tourist is caught in a constant and inescapable dilemma: he or she is there to see, to capture the authenticity of the object in a moment of individual self-development. But he or she is caught in the fact that tourism is a mass spectacle, that he or she is only one of many tourists who have passed this way for the 'view,' that, indeed, those other tourists may well be blocking the view and rendering impossible the solitary experience. This dilemma – to be superior to the 'tourists' while at once recognizing one's kinship with them – is what is solved by Bond, the ideal tourist, always alone and always superior. His tourism has an ostensible purpose, though the line between tourism and spying is a fine one.

Tourism and touristic ways of seeing are not only inscribed in Fleming's prose but also organize what might be called the Fleming 'world system,' a world system dependant upon Cold War and imperialist ideologies but not entirely congruent with them. For the setting of the Bond books is not entirely established either by the Cold War axis of East and West – to which England is not central – nor by the imperialist axis of British metropolis and colonial periphery. Rather it is established in large part by what Louis Turner and John Ash have termed the 'pleasure

periphery,' the tourist belt surrounding the industrialized
world including the Mediterranean, the Caribbean, the
Philippines, Hong Kong, Indonesia.[15] Much of this world is
dependent upon the neo-colonialism of the tourist industry;
it stands, for Bond, as an idyllic paradise, as a more authentic culture, and as a source of threat and upheaval.

As an idyllic paradise, these locations are the settings for
sports, elaborate meals, and sexual adventure. The women
who are 'out-of-place sexually,' 'deviant' politically or sexually in that they are in league with the villain or are
lesbians, are encountered in these 'pleasure peripheries,'
and it is here, away from Miss Moneypenny and May,
Bond's 'treasured Scottish housekeeper,' that Bond is free to
battle, seduce, and then retreat to London. These women, as
their names indicate (Pussy Galore, Tiffany Case, Honeychilde Rider, Kissy Suzuki), are apparently outside of the
British sex/gender system entirely (though we will examine
this more closely in the next section); they are part of the
'view.' Here Fleming's setting is not far from the tourist
advertisements of a holiday in the sun.

The second meaning of these settings invokes a more
complex version of tourism, the viewing of a more vital,
more authentic culture. For tourism has often meant the
encounter with another, non-capitalist (or non-monopoly
capitalist) mode of production with its kinship structures,
its handicrafts, its street life and marketplaces. And here
Bond is given a more privileged access than the average
tourist. He is taken, by his secret work, into secret worlds –
the Harlem of Mr. Big in *Live and Let Die*, the Jamaica of
Dr. No, and the Istanbul of Kerim in *From Russia, With
Love*. These are the environs of the grotesque Fleming
villains, who are, as Eco has shown, usually of mixed blood,
obscure origins, abnormal sexuality, and physical mon-
strosity, and work in obscure alliances with the KGB. But
they are also the home of those figures that we might call,
after Propp, the donors: the characters – quintessentially
Kerim in *From Russia, With Love* and Quarrel in *Dr. No* –
with whom Bond makes indispensable alliances, alliances
that allow him access to the non-Western cultures and

therefore give him the strength to defeat the villain on his home territory. Darko Kerim, for example, who heads the secret service's Istanbul office, mediates England and Turkey, having a Turkish father and an English mother. His knowledge of the territory is indispensable to Bond; he serves as a kind of tour guide not only to the presence of the Russians but also to the clubs and taverns of Istanbul. The visit to a gipsy restaurant leads to a supper with the gipsies and to Bond's witnessing a fight between two gipsy women, the settling of a family affair. As Kerim says to Bond, 'It will not be for the squeamish, but it will be a remarkable affair. It is a great privilege that we may be present. You understand? We are *gajos* [foreigners]. You will forget your sense of proprieties? You will not interfere? They will kill you, and possibly me, if you did.'[16] This is a tourist's view beyond that of the Bosphorus, a view of an 'older,' more thorough patriarchy, a fight between two women of the 'tribe' over the rights to the son, supervised by the father. It is a patriarchy that is seen in a less crude form in Kerim himself, all of whose operatives are sons. This world is seen as being surpassed – Kerim will be killed – but its secrets are needed by Bond, who has only the metaphoric institutional father, M.

But this world is also a threatening world to Bond. *Dr. No* opens in Jamaica, where Fleming himself lived, and the narrator writes of the mansion that houses Kingston 'Society': 'Such stubborn retreats will not survive long in modern Jamaica. One day Queen's Club will have its windows smashed and perhaps be burned to the ground, but for the time being it is a useful place to find in a sub-tropical island – well run, well staffed and with the finest cuisine and cellar in the Caribbean.'[17] This sense of doom comes from the shadow of a real history hanging over the stories. The grotesque villains, each defeated in turn, are avatars of a more profound threat to the wellbeing, not only of England or the West, but of the tourist. We can mark this objectively as decolonization, the emergence of the character of the 'Third World' as the result of protracted liberation struggles throughout Asia, Africa, and Latin America. Frantz Fanon has written that the psychic equivalent of decolonization is the reversal of the look, the refusal to be the object of the colonizer's gaze. And this indeed is the anxiety of the tourist: as Felix Leiter, Bond's American helper, says to Bond: 'Harlem's a bit of a jungle these days. People don't go up there anymore like they used to . . . One used to go to the Savoy Ballroom and watch the dancing . . . Now that's all changed. Harlem doesn't like being stared at anymore.' A little later, 'Bond suddenly felt the force of what Leiter had told him. They were trespassing. They just weren't wanted.'[18] The narrative of tourism here finds its limits; Bond's licence to look is revoked.

For Your Eyes Only

> But the new prominence of sex in the late Fifties was not just a concern with the realities of sex; even more, it was a preoccupation with the idea of sex, the image of sex; the written image, the visual image, the image that was promulgated in advertisements, in increasingly 'daring' films, in 'controversial' newspaper articles and 'frank' novels; the image purveyed by the strip-tease clubs and pornographic book shops that were springing up in the back streets of Soho and provincial cities; and the image that, mixed with that of violence, was responsible in the years after 1956 for the enormous boom in the sales of Ian Fleming's James Bond stories.
>
> – Christopher Booker, *The Neophiliacs* (1969)

Probably the most striking innovation of the thrillers of Ian Fleming for contemporary readers lay in their codes of sexuality. Both critics and enthusiasts of James Bond focused on his sexual adventures; they all noted that the Bond tales were the first British thrillers to make sexual encounters central to the plot and to the hero. The thrillers of Buchan, Sapper, and Ambler all avoided anything but the most fleeting accounts of sexual relations, and whatever erotic energy they had was covert or displaced into other codes, particularly into representations of violence and torture. Nevertheless, striking as this shift seemed to contemporary readers and reviewers, one wonders about its meaning. For the sexual politics of the Bond thrillers are in many ways very traditional, and the representations of sexuality are, by the conventions of the 1980s, tame. The apparent novelty of Bond was, one might conclude, another version of a persistent and recurrent masculine fantasy dressed up in the latest fashions of a consumer society. This is the view taken by Tony Bennett in his illuminating discussion of the 'sexist code' in the Bond narratives, which details how the plots work to reposition a woman who is 'out-of-place' sexually and politically into a traditional ordering of sexual difference. As an example he cites Bond's view of the recent history of gender:

> Bond came to the conclusion that Tilly Masterton was one of those girls whose hormones had got mixed up. He knew the type well and thought they and their male counterparts were a direct consequence of giving votes to women and 'sex equality'. As a result of fifty years of emancipation, feminine qualities were dying out or being transferred to the males. Pansies of both sexes were everywhere, not yet completely homosexual, but confused, not knowing what they were. The result was a herd of unhappy sexual misfits – barren and full of frustrations, the women wanting to dominate and the men to be nannied. He was sorry for them, but he had no time for them.

Faced with this world, Bond's mission is to 'rescue' these women, to re-establish order in the world of gender. And he has few doubts as to the nature of that order, as one sees in this passage from *Casino Royale*:

> He sighed. Women were for recreation. On a job they got in the way and fogged things up with sex and hurt feelings and all the emotional baggage they carried around. One had to look out for them and take care of them. 'Bitch,' said Bond . . .[19]

Yet the very crudeness of Fleming's fantasies of male

power should not obscure their historical specificity; nor should the manifest absurdity of Bond's history of gender in the twentieth-century lead us to forget Bond's place in the history of gender. For *Casino Royale* (1953) takes its place alongside *Playboy* (1953) as the mark of the first mass pornography. To say this is to define pornography not simply as a depiction of male power (in which case it surely predated Bond or *Playboy*) nor as any particular representation of sexuality (for the conventions of these representations change over time and the conventions of both Bond and the 1950s *Playboy* now scarcely qualify as pornographic); rather what characterizes these representations and the era of mass pornography are, first, a narrative structured around the look, the voyeuristic eye, coding *woman* as its object, and second, a culture whose every discourse is dominated by, indeed translated into, a code of sexual signifiers.

The argument that pornography is better defined as a version of voyeurism than as a representation of sexuality is drawn in part from the fact that much of what passes as pornography is not the representation of sexual activities but the representation of women's bodies in various states of undress. Thus, as Annette Kuhn puts it, 'in an address to male spectators, the body of woman is constructed as a spectacle and the *mise en scène* of representations of women's bodies coded in various ways as both to be looked at by the spectator and, in the same process, to evoke sexual arousal in him.' This line of thought owes much to Laura Mulvey's important essay which attempted to show how the classic Hollywood cinema constructs woman as an object of looking and constructs the spectator as male. The conclusion that Kuhn draws, a conclusion that is central to an understanding of James Bond, is that pornography is not exceptional, not qualitatively different from other representations in the culture. Rather pornography occupies 'one point on a continuum of representations of women, a continuum along which are also situated such commonly available and highly socially visible representations as advertisements.'[20] Thus, the James Bond tales can rightly be seen as an important early form of the mass pornography that characterizes the consumer society, the society of the spectacle, that emerges in Western Europe and North America in the wake of post-war reconstruction.

For Bond's pornographic imagination is structured not so much around explicit depictions of sexual acts as around Bond as voyeur, Bond as spy. We see this in the scene where Bond first encounters Honeychilde Rider:

> It was a naked girl, with her back to him. She was not quite naked. She wore a broad leather belt around her waist with a hunting knife in a leather sheath at her right hip. The belt made her nakedness extraordinarily erotic. She stood not more than five yards away on the tideline looking down at something in her hand. She stood in the classical relaxed pose of the nude, all the weight on the right leg and the left knee bent and turning slightly inwards, the head to one side as she examined the things in her hand.[21]

This picture of Bond the voyeur is related, of course, to the tourist Bond; but it also structures the actions of Bond the secret agent.

If we take *From Russia, With Love* as an example, we can see how the permutations of the voyeur, of Bond's licence to look, organize a series of loosely connected, virtuoso anecdotes that make up the heart of Bond's adventures in Istanbul. Bond's first action after arriving and taking in the 'view' is to accompany Kerim through an underground tunnel in order to spy on the Russian Embassy through a periscope; it is through this periscope that he first glimpses Tatiana Romanova, the Russian filing clerk who has supposedly fallen in love with his photograph. This episode is followed by the celebrated scene, entitled 'Strong Sensations,' in which Bond, together with Kerim, watches the fight between the gipsy women: 'Bond held his breath at the sight of the two glistening, naked bodies, and he could feel Kerim's body tense beside him. The ring of gipsies seemed to have come closer to the two fighters. The moon shone on the glittering eyes and there was the whisper of hot, panting breath.' Since Bond is pledged, as a tourist, not to interfere with the women, this scene ends in an orgy of gunfire only tangentially related to the plot. The assassination of Krilencu follows this episode; but what is memorable here is not the assassination but its location, the 'mouth of Marilyn Monroe':

> 'Sniperscope. German model,' whispered Kerim. 'Infra-red lens. Sees in the dark. Have a look at that big film advertisement over there. That face. Just below the nose. You'll see the outline of a trap door.' . . . Bond rested his forearm against the door jamb and raised the tube to his right eye . . . The outline of a huge woman's face and some lettering appeared . . . Bond inched the glass down the vast pile of Marilyn Monroe's hair, and the cliff of forehead, and down the two feet of nose to the cavernous nostrils. A faint square showed in the poster. It ran from below the nose into the great alluring curve of the lips . . . Out of the mouth of the huge, shadowed poster, between the great violet lips, half open in ecstasy, the dark shape of a man emerged and hung down like a worm from the mouth of a corpse.

The sight of Krilencu is dwarfed by the look of the spectacle, doubly magnified: the voyeur Bond with the Sniperscope, the pin-up as a grotesque but alluring poster. Bond only watches the assassin, Kerim; indeed, the narrator informs us that Bond has never killed in cold blood. Bond's licence to kill is here clearly less important than his licence to look.[22]

Bond then returns to his hotel to find the compliant Tatiana Romanova, naked in his bed; but this final episode of his Istanbul adventures has an ironic twist. Rather than an explicit representation of Bond and Tatiana in bed, the spy Bond is spied upon, and the reader finds himself sharing a view with SMERSH itself:

> Above them, and unknown to both of them, behind the gold-framed false mirror on the wall over the bed, the

two photographers from SMERSH sat close together
in the cramped cabinet de voyeur, as, before them, so
many friends of the proprietor had sat on a honeymoon
night in the stateroom of the Kristal Palas. And the
viewfinders gazed coldly down on the passionate
arabesques the two bodies formed and broke and
formed again, and the clockwork mechanism of the
cine-cameras whirred softly on and on as the breath
rasped out of the open mouths of the two men and the
sweat of excitement trickled down their bulging faces
into their cheap collars.

These films are part of the Soviet plot to destroy the image
of Bond.[23]

This brief account of Bond's adventures in Istanbul
shows the ways in which the presence of sexuality manifests
itself in figures of looking, in spying and being spied upon.
But this does not account for the historical specificity of
these figures; surely, the dynamics of voyeurism predate the
appearance of James Bond, as much as they contribute to
his success. The novelty is signaled by the poster of Marilyn
Monroe; the object of the gaze is not a woman but a
commodified image, an image from the world of film. Thus
the novelty of the Bond tales, and that of mass-produced
pornography generally, is its place in the new organization
of sexuality in consumer capitalism. This takes two forms.
On the one hand, one of the characteristics of consumer
capitalism is, as the social theorist Herbert Marcuse pointed
out, the libidinalization of the workplace and daily life,
what he termed 'repressive desublimation.'[24] In this situation, sexuality becomes the master code into which all
discourses – commercial, political, philosophical, even religious – are translated. And just as a society which translated
all economic, political, and philosophical discourse into a
religious code found its ideological boundaries defined and
contested in terms of heresy, so this consumer capitalism
which relentlessly transcodes politics, religion, and philosophy into sexual terms fights its ideological battles under the
sign of pornography. These battles are not, despite appear-

ances, merely battles between the forces of 'liberation' and the forces of 'repression.' The apparent liberation of sexuality from patriarchal norms – the so-called 'sexual revolution' – is both a genuine change in sexual practices and a reconstitution of sexuality in a fetishized mode that continues to subordinate and oppress women. Nevertheless there is a kinship between the appearance of Bond and *Playboy* and the celebrated trials of *Lady Chatterley's Lover* and the works of Henry Miller. Indeed, John Sutherland tells us that the 'paperback revolution' arrived in Britain with the mass sales of the Bond books *and* the mass sales of these literary works the libraries wouldn't carry.

But the other part of the reorganization of sexuality in consumer capitalism is tied to a shift in the sex/gender system itself, that contradictory combination of a particular sexual division of labor and certain dominant sexual ideologies. The new sex/gender system which has emerged in consumer society has yet to be named fully, but it is characterized by the expansion and industrialization of the service sector with its largely female workforce, the creation of a sexual market less marked by the formal institutions of marriage and prostitution, and the demise of the family wage system; this has generated an ideological revolt by men against the 'breadwinner ethic,' the self-organization of women in the feminist movement, and indeed the construction of a new culture, a culture that might be figured in the names *Playboy* and *Cosmopolitan*.[25] It is in this context that the sexuality and masculinity of Bond appears: a masculinity defined by freedom from marriage, an easy familiarity with the brand names that are the accompaniments to a consumer lifestyle – cars, cigarettes, liquor – and a licence to look.

5

Looking-glass wars

If books could kill: from thriller to spy novel

Ian Fleming's *From Russia, With Love* comes to its climax on a train going through the Simplon Tunnel in a bizarre battle of books. Bond is sharing a compartment with 'Captain Nash,' supposedly a British agent but actually the Soviet assassin Red Grant. As they approach the tunnel, they are two ordinary travelers, Nash reading Tolstoy's *War and Peace* and Bond reading Eric Ambler's *The Mask of Dimitrios*. Suddenly, Nash shoots Bond in the wrist with his book, a disguised gun. 'Too bad that book of yours is only for reading, old man,' Nash jokes. But Bond, ever alert, slips his cigarette case between the pages of his Ambler, and, when Nash's book fires again for his heart, Bond saves himself with his own reinforced book. He then grabs the copy of *War and Peace* – 'The book! How did one work the thing?' – and kills Nash.[1]

This scene is not only a virtuoso Bond ending but is also an amusing allegory of a wider battle of books, with the plucky English thriller besting the powerful Russian work of literature. And though Bond, like Fleming, is not quite sure how *War and Peace* works, he makes do, turning Tolstoy to the service of the thriller. This little game that Fleming plays is more interesting when we realize that the

packaging of the early Fleming novels wrapped them up as
'literary' thrillers. They were published in hardcover by
Jonathan Cape, and were reviewed in the literary weeklies:
Fleming himself defined them as 'thrillers designed to be
read as literature.'[2] And though they have long since fallen
(or risen) to the mass market (defined at first by their
appearance as Pan paperbacks), they retain a certain play-
fulness and self-consciousness about their own status as
artifacts.

With Fleming, the thriller becomes the 'spy novel' in two
new and contrary senses, both of which make for this
self-consciousness. The first move is toward the 'literary,'
the spy *novel*; the second, toward the generic, the *spy* novel.
For though Fleming's self-consciousness and occasional
self-referentiality is not too far from the language play of
post-modernism, perhaps the point is not that Fleming is a
post-modernist, but rather that there is a transformation in
popular fiction that corresponds to the post-modernist
moment in high culture: I will call this 'genre fiction' to
suggest that the extreme division of popular fiction into
narrow and commercially defined 'genres' – Westerns, spy
thrillers, detective stories, Mills & Boon romances (or
Harlequins in North America), science fiction – is a comparatively recent event which can be dated from the specializa-
tion of pulp magazines (which had been general 'all-story'
magazines) in the 1920s and the first fetishization of a
popular genre in the codification of the 'rules' of the detective tale in the late 1920s.[3] These highly codified genres lead
also to the playful forms of intertextuality that we find in
Fleming and other 'genre' writers, the allusions to other
writers and books within the genre. This emergence of
highly coded discrete genres also helps explain why I have a
much harder time defining a spy thriller before the advent of
Fleming than after, and indeed why this study is itself
largely defined by a particular reified popular genre.

But if Bond and his formulaic followers – William Haggard's Colonel Charles Russell, James Leasor's Dr. Jason
Love, James Dark's Mark Hood, Philip McCutchan's Com-
mander Shaw, and John Gardner's Boysie Oakes (and later,

Gardner's revival of James Bond) – define a certain entity, the mass-produced (often paperback original) spy novel, in a way in which it had never really existed before, the tales of espionage of John le Carré, Len Deighton, and Graham Greene moved the thriller further toward the 'literary' and established the 'spy novel' as a mainstay of middlebrow fiction. As LeRoy Panek has written, 'the golden age of the spy novel began in the early 1960s, and it has lasted for twenty years . . . During this period the spy novel separated itself decisively from the thriller.'[4] It is this period that I will look at in this chapter.

John Sutherland has called the period since 1944 in the world of the fiction industry the age of Graham Greene. In many ways Greene sums up many of the tendencies Sutherland notes: the resurgence of the realist novel in the wake of an attenuated British modernism, the patronage of the British novelist by the expanded post-war public library system, the international themes and settings demanded by the international Anglophone audience (Sutherland says that Greene has five to ten American purchasers for every English one[5]), and the interest in popular genre fiction like the thriller. Greene, after all, accompanied his 'novels' of the 1930s and 1940s with the series of 'entertainments,' the spy thrillers that, along with those of Eric Ambler, changed the nature of the thriller: *Stamboul Train, The Confidential Agent, A Gun for Sale, The Ministry of Fear*. So it is not surprising that Greene is one of the most self-conscious spy writers. In *The Human Factor* (1978), his return to the genre, Greene tells his own 'battle of the books,' a somewhat more low-key one than that of Fleming, in his allegory of the two bookshops. The narrator tells us that there are two bookshops facing each other on Old Compton Street in Soho. The one owned by Halliday Sr. is a respectable bookshop 'full of Penguins and Everyman and second-hand copies of World's Classics'; across the street is a pornography shop owned by Halliday Jr. Castle's contact with the Soviets is Halliday Jr., but for reasons of security and Castle's own respectability, the father passes the messages back and forth. Or so Castle believes. The surprise comes when Castle is about to escape to Moscow and he discovers that his contact is really Halliday Sr. One reading of this little allegory, if that is what it is, would be that this book, *The Human Factor*, which the reader thinks is an entertainment, a thriller, is really a serious novel, a second-hand World's Classic. And indeed, whereas in a period of high modernism Greene accepted the split between World's Classics and thrillers by sorting his own work into 'novels' and 'entertainments,' he has now dropped that distinction. In an interview, Greene has said, 'I established the distinction originally to escape "melodrama". (I've subsequently concluded that melodrama isn't all that baneful) . . . The last one to be conceived in this category was *The Ministry of Fear*: after that novels and entertainments resembled each other more and more.' *The Human Factor* is clearly a 'novel' written with the materials of an 'entertainment.' And here we find, once again, *War and Peace*, now being used by the double agent Castle for his book codes: 'Castle began reading in Book II of *War and Peace*. It was a breach of security, even a small act of defiance, to read this book publicly for pleasure.'[6]

The shift that began this golden age of the spy *novel* was marked by the publication in 1962 of Len Deighton's *The Ipcress File* and in 1963 of John le Carré's *The Spy Who Came in from the Cold*. Both writers came of age after World War II, and reconstructed the thriller in the face of the Cold War, the Suez Crisis of 1956, and decolonization. So I will begin by looking at the way these stories of owls and moles became a powerful explanation of the end of Empire. But these were also cover stories of white-collar work, of the organization man, and as such they were to find a new readership throughout the English-speaking world, giving a new and unprecedented cultural importance to stories of espionage. And the figures who loomed over these looking-glass wars of 'cold warriors,' civil servants, and corporate managers were George Smiley and Kim Philby.

'Or would you rather be Swiss?': the ideology of Englishness

> All power corrupts. The loss of power corrupts even more.
> We can thank an American for that advice. It's quite true.
> We are a corrupt nation, and we need all the help we can get.
> That is lamentable and, I confess, occasionally humiliating.
> However, I would rather fail as a power than survive by
> impotence. I would rather be vanquished than neutral. I
> would rather be English than Swiss.
>
> — Bradfield to Turner, in John le Carré's
> *A Small Town in Germany* (1968)

The story of Kim Philby is a cover story in more ways than
one. It began with his own cover story, hiding for almost
thirty years the fact he was a Soviet spy. It then became a
cover-up, in which the British government first exonerated
Philby, and then, after his flight to Moscow, attempted to
suppress the entire affair. When the newspapers ignored the
D-notices (a sort of government recommendation of self-
censorship), it became a cover story in *The Times* and the
Observer. And it was then taken up by a number of
novelists including the two I will concentrate on in this
chapter, John le Carré in his *Tinker, Tailor, Soldier, Spy*
(1974) and Graham Greene in *The Human Factor* (1978).

There are several plots in the Kim Philby case. The cover
story of Kim Philby's career went something like this: the
young Philby, graduate of Cambridge in the 1930s, covers
the Spanish Civil War as a journalist, enters the British
secret service in 1940, and moves up to become the head of
the newly created section dealing with intelligence about the
Soviet Union in 1944. In 1951, two Foreign Office officials,
Guy Burgess and Donald Maclean, flee to Moscow, just as
they are about to be revealed as Soviet agents. In the furor
that follows, Philby is asked to resign because of his
friendship with Burgess. Philby returns to journalism and,
in 1955, in response to questions, Harold Macmillan, the
Foreign Secretary, states in the House of Commons that
there is no evidence that Philby had betrayed the interests of

Britain. In 1956, Philby goes as a journalist to Beirut, where he stays until January 1963, when he leaves for the Soviet Union. In July 1963, the government announces that Philby was the 'third man' in the Burgess and Maclean affair and had been a Soviet agent.

The actual story of Philby, which began to be revealed in a series of alternative plots published after 1963, goes more like this: Philby becomes a Communist at Cambridge, though he never joins the party, witnesses the destruction of the Austrian socialists in 1934, and is recruited in England as a Soviet agent. His work as a Soviet agent does not fully conflict with his work in the British secret service until after World War II. He seems to have betrayed the invasion of Albania in 1949, helped break down Anglo-American relations, and tipped off Burgess and Maclean. After being cleared by Macmillan, he rejoins the British secret service under the cover of a journalist. He is also reactivated as a Soviet agent. The defection of a KGB officer in 1962 betrays Philby and he flees to Moscow.[7]

However, the Philby narrative is more complex than its events. Philby was a member of Britain's Establishment. His father, St. John Philby, was an Arabist, one time imperial servant, and explorer of the Saudi Desert: a figure of the Empire, like his more famous contemporary, T.E. Lawrence. Kim received the education appropriate to his class, at Westminster School followed by Trinity College, Cambridge. He assumed the characteristics of a recognizable type: the gentleman eccentric with his epicureanism, his associations with homosexuals, and his heavy drinking. As John le Carré wrote in an essay on Philby: 'Effortlessly he played the parts which the establishment could recognize — for was he not born and trained into the establishment! Effortlessly he copied its attitudes, caught its diffident stammer, its hesitant arrogance; effortlessly he took his place in its nameless hegemony.' And so his betrayal was a trauma; he was, as le Carré writes, 'of our blood and hunted with our pack.'[8]

But it was not simply that a member of the Establishment had been unmasked as a spy; rather the revelation was part of the coming into public consciousness of the Establishment itself – indeed, of the figuration of the ruling class as the 'Establishment.' It has been claimed that the word was first used 'during the Burgess and Maclean revelations in September 1955; [a journalist] alleged that the two diplomats had been "protected" by the Establishment.' 'The Establishment,' Hugh Thomas wrote in a popular tract of 1959, 'is the present-day institutional museum of Britain's past greatness. Consider first the Public Schools . . . the whole slant of public school education is to provide a continuous stream of socially gifted and athletic amateurs to act as pro-consuls in, however, an Empire that no longer exists today.'[9] The case of the 'missing diplomats' was a breach in the notion of 'service,' and in the attendant ideas of amateurism and loyalty, that had served as a justification of the hegemony of that ruling class. Raymond Williams, writing in 1958, counterposed 'the idea of service, which is the great achievement of the Victorian middle class, and is deeply inherited by its successors,' to the earlier idea of *laissez-faire* individualism, and to the idea of solidarity, developed in the working-class movement. He writes:

A very large part of English middle class education is devoted to the training of servants. This is much more its characteristic than a training for leadership, as the stress on conformity and on respect for authority shows. In so far as it is, by definition, the training of upper servants, it includes, of course, the instilling of that kind of confidence which will enable the upper servants to supervise and direct the lower servants . . . Yet the upper servant is not to think of his own interests. He must subordinate these to a larger good, which is called the Queen's peace, or national security, or law and order, or the public weal. This has been the charter of many thousands of devoted lives, and it is necessary to respect it even where we cannot agree with it . . . It seems to me inadequate because in practice it serves, at every level, to maintain and confirm the *status quo*.[10]

Philby, of course, worked for the secret *service*. The narrative of Kim Philby is one of the betrayal of the service and the idea of service; it is the riddle and cover-up of the question 'who killed Great Britain?'

The answers to that question began coming in the late 1950s, soon after the Suez Crisis, and continued through the next two decades. Andrew Gamble, in his *Britain in Decline*, notes that the early 1960s saw a flood of self-criticism, finding scapegoats for Britain's ills in the civil service, the unions, the City, and the managers, but particularly in the 'anti-enterprise' and anti-scientific culture of service and amateurism.[11] Answers from a new left appeared in such documents as the *Out of Apathy* collection of 1960, Raymond Williams's *The Long Revolution* (1961), and Perry Anderson's 'Origins of the Present Crisis' (1964). And the new 'cynical' spy novels were not only symptoms of this crisis of confidence but accounts of its origins; this is particularly true of the novels that meditate on the figure of Kim Philby. In looking at these novels I will begin with their historical inaccuracies, displacements, and rewritings, not in order to judge the novels by their fidelity to the documented facts, but to see those differences as loci of meaning. This is illuminating even when no historical accuracy is intended; for though both le Carré and Greene have written essays on Philby, neither wrote novels about him; both, however, meditated on the Philby myth, and on its continuing resonances.

Before turning to le Carré and Greene, however, let me briefly mention two other spy novels written about Philby. Alan Williams's *Gentleman Traitor* (1974) is explicitly about a character named Kim Philby; Dorothea Bennett's *The Jigsaw Man* (1976) is about a loosely disguised character named Philip Kimberly. They are both competently written, average spy thrillers: 'good reads.' They are very different books: Bennett's focuses on romance, dealing with the love affair of Philip Kimberly's daughter; Williams's novel, in its best parts, is about 'terrorism' against white Rhodesians. What they share is what I'll call the weak misreading of the Philby story, a simple wish fulfillment:

Philby grows disillusioned with the Soviet Union, repents, and comes back. As a plot device it might be interesting: the double agent doubles back. But neither book is convincing, and one senses that the authors themselves are not fully convinced. For in order to rehabilitate Philby, both find it necessary to reveal another Englishman, a lord, as a Soviet agent.

In Greene and le Carré there is none of this. There are no Philip Kimberlys, no loosely disguised stand-ins. Indeed, Greene goes so far as to claim that he abandoned his novel for a period because of the Philby case: 'My double agent, Maurice Castle, bore no resemblance in character or motive to Philby, . . . [and] I disliked the idea of the novel being taken as a *roman à clef*.'[12] What is left is the bare bones: the story of the revelation of a 'mole,' a double agent, in the British secret service. Le Carré's *Tinker, Tailor, Soldier, Spy* (1974) was his fourth spy novel, the first of a trilogy (followed by *The Honourable Schoolboy* and *Smiley's People*) in which the enigmatic figure of George Smiley moved to the foreground. Le Carré's first spy novel, *The Spy Who Came in from the Cold* (1963), marked a 'realist' trumping of the James Bond novels of the 1950s with its cold, spare and cynical prose; beginning and ending at the Berlin Wall, it is one of the great war novels of the Cold War. *Tinker, Tailor, Soldier, Spy* is the story of a double revenge, with two centers of consciousness: Smiley, 'small, podgy, and at best middle-aged,' a donnish cuckold; and Jim Prideaux, the young athletic adventurer with a 'passionate Englishness.' A débâcle in Czechoslovakia before the book opens has led to a changeover in the Circus, the secret service. Control has died in disgrace; Smiley, his right-hand man, has been forced to retire and is now estranged from his wife; Jim, the agent in Czechoslovakia, has been wounded and is now teaching in a seedy public school. A love affair in Hong Kong between an Australian gunrunner, Tarr, and a Soviet courier, Irana, leads to the information, confirming Smiley's suspicions, that there is a mole high in the Circus who betrayed the Czech operation. Smiley is brought back from retirement by the government to investigate the Circus as an outsider. He then visits in turn the former Circus members who have been betrayed and dismissed, exchanging his faith in them for their knowledge, finally meeting with Jim Prideaux. Armed with this knowledge, Smiley sets a trap for the mole and catches him. He turns out to be Bill Haydon, the golden boy, 'our latter-day Lawrence of Arabia,' who has been the lover of Smiley's wife, Ann, and of Jim Prideaux. Haydon confesses and is mysteriously killed, though there is evidence that the old lover, Jim, did it.

The Human Factor (1978) marked Graham Greene's return to the spy thriller, a genre he had helped create in his 'entertainments' of the 1930s, and had then largely abandoned. It is the story of Maurice Castle, a punctual, efficient civil servant who 'daydreams of complete conformity.' The discovery of a leak in the African section of the secret service leads to the entrance of Daintry, the security officer, and an investigation of Castle and his co-worker Arthur Davis. Daintry sees inconclusive evidence pointing to Davis, but rather than investigate further, his superior kills Davis. It is a providential death for Castle, who is revealed by the narrator as the double agent, serving the Soviets because they had helped his black wife out of South Africa. The discovery of the leak and the elimination of Davis means that Castle must stop leaking information or be caught. At this point, Cornelius Muller of South African intelligence, Castle's old enemy, enters. Castle decides to send to the Soviets news of Uncle Remus, a US–Britain–South Africa plan to use atomic weapons. When the man he thinks is his Soviet contact is arrested, Castle prepares to leave. Daintry, upset over the mistaken killing of Davis, reports Castle's guilt and resigns. Castle flees to Moscow, and is left separated from his wife and child at the end of the book.

Those are the plots. Some differences are striking. Though both are third-person narratives, Greene writes mainly from the consciousness of the mole, Castle. The emphasis is entirely on his motives; the Philby case is reconstructed in the context of contemporary African politics to make those motives more understandable and more sympathetic. And Castle betrays only a firm; he is a nobody, certainly not a figure for the ruling class or the Empire. It is true that his Cambridge background exempts him from suspicion at first; Davis is suspected because he studied at Reading. The investigator Daintry is also as much a loner in the bureaucracy as those he hunts.

Le Carré, on the other hand, is interested in who the betrayer is and what was betrayed; his is a story of the best and the brightest. Haydon is clearly a figure for the ruling class, for past glory as well as present shame. Le Carré is not really interested in motives; like his hero Smiley, he distrusts 'the standard shape of human motives.' Nevertheless, le Carré uses the somewhat discredited Muggeridge thesis about Philby in constructing Haydon — that he was a genuine pro-fascist in the 1930s and joined the Russians in the 1940s, rather than that his pro-fascist activities were a cover for his Soviet work, as Philby himself claims.[13]

The difference in emphasis may come, I think, from the slightly different positions of Greene and le Carré in English society. Greene, as a Catholic, has always put himself on the outside; and by an analogy of Catholicism and Communism he can justify (in his essay on Philby) Philby in his own terms, comparing Philby with the Elizabethan Catholics who worked for the victory of Catholic Spain. He further compares Philby in the face of Stalin with a Catholic during the Inquisition: 'If there was a Torquemada now, he would have known in his heart that one day there would be a John XXIII.'[14] So Castle betrays England because he is a 'naturalized black,' and has allegiances that transcend nationality.

Le Carré, on the other hand, stands on the inside: 'Philby's is one of those cases which force us to define our own place in society. I suppose by "we" I mean the world to which I myself vaguely belong: middle-class, graduate, intellectual. Philby's world, but indoors.'[15] So his Smiley is one who 'shared *everything* once upon a time' with the traitor Haydon; and Smiley realizes at the end that they all tacitly knew Haydon was the mole and all refused to acknowledge it to themselves.

But in another way *The Human Factor* and *Tinker, Tailor, Soldier, Spy* are very similar books, and I will turn to

Fredric Jameson's notion of a character system to explore this similarity. Jameson develops this character system out of A.J. Greimas's semantic rectangle and it is, as Jameson admits, 'a forbidding apparatus.' But it may be used in the analysis of narrative as a way of avoiding a simple notion of characters as 'real people,' as substances, by seeing characters as products of systems of relations.[16]

The semantic rectangle can also prevent us from being locked into any binary opposition by positing the other terms implied by it. The importance of this for an analysis of popular fiction can be seen by comparing Umberto Eco's account of Ian Fleming's James Bond novels with Jameson's analysis of a science fiction novel by Philip K. Dick.[17] Eco uses the tool of the binary opposition to penetrate the Bond novels; he catalogs the various oppositions found – Bond/Villain, Free World/Soviet Union, Moderation/Excess – and concludes that Fleming has a Manichean ideology, and that this Manicheism, programed into the narratives, accounts for the particular racist and anti-Communist ideologies. This may well be the case with Fleming, but one wonders if the strict 'binarization' of all elements of the novels in the name of analysis did not in some way program his conclusion.

Jameson's use of the semantic rectangle in the analysis of Dick's *Dr. Bloodmoney*, on the other hand, allows him to avoid simple binaries of the type 'Bond/Villain' and to see characters as combinations of semes (units of meaning) – semes which are organized by relations of opposition and negation. Thus he can show how the story generates a mediating figure which unites both terms of, for example, the contraries of 'organic/mechanical.'

Many critics have noted that the opposition between 'Good' and 'Evil' is central to the thriller.[18] Here Eco's account of the Bond stories as narrativizations of the Manichean ideology which sees the world in terms of a constant struggle between Good and Evil is to some degree persuasive. Even Jameson seems to see the Bond novels in this way, since he sees the anti-Bond thriller as a simple reversal: 'the theological thriller, as it plays itself out from Greene to le

Carré, proposed a simple but effective reversal, in which it is the villains (Graham Greene's sinful, guilt-ridden Catholics, le Carré's East Germans) who turn out to embody the positive term, while the stereotypical heroes (healthy athletic Protestants or clean cut American Cold Warriors) are unmasked as the agents of evil and human suffering.'[19]

If, however, we see the novels in terms of the semantic rectangle, both Bond and the 'theological thriller' shift somewhat. First we see that the Good/Evil contrary is most often articulated as a England/Communist polarity (I say Communist rather than Soviet Union because the long tradition of German villains in English fiction often displaces the Communist villains from the USSR to East Germany).

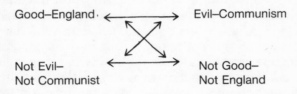

Second, it seems that the 'not Communist' place is usually filled by the non-Communist Americans, and that the not-England place often becomes the non-imperialists, the colonial and ex-colonial world. So, for example in the Bond stories, there is usually a fairly simple struggle between Bond and his American helper (Felix Leiter, in *Live and Let Die* and others), and the Communists in an Eastern or colonial setting (the black Jamaican Communist, Mr. Big, in *Live and Let Die*, for example). Even in Fleming, though, the figures that are most interesting are those that mediate between the ideological contraries, uniting Good and Evil in equivocal and ambiguous ways: for example, in *From Russia, With Love*, the center of gravity shifts from Bond/ Villain to Kerim, Bond's Turkish helper, and to Red Grant, the British born and raised Soviet assassin.

In both *Tinker, Tailor, Soldier, Spy* and *The Human Factor* this mediating figure is clear: he is the double agent, the object of the novel's search. But if one looks more closely at our rectangle one can begin to see the way the logic of Good and Evil becomes a narrative, generating and explaining the mediating figure. For the shift of the two double agents from Good to Evil, from England to the Communists, is accomplished by the emergence of the simple negations (the not-English, not-Communist) into positive contraries. So when the Americans develop from the non-Communist helper in the Bond stories to a positive anti-Communist force, le Carré's mole moves from one side of the rectangle to the other. I have said that le Carré is not terribly interested in motives; but when he does account for Haydon's motives it is entirely in terms of the US. Early in the novel Haydon refers to the 'Fascist puritans of the American agency,' and he is contrasted to the head of the Circus, Alleline, who 'always had a fatal reverence for the Americans.' Haydon said he himself 'hated America very deeply, and Smiley supposed he did.' Haydon's early work for the Russians consisted of betraying not England but the American secrets England possessed.[20]

In *The Human Factor*, it is the other negation, the non-imperialist, which becomes a positive contrary: the anti-imperialist, anti-colonialist Africa. Castle betrays England and switches sides of the rectangle because of his allegiance to his black African wife, Sarah. He had become, he says, 'a naturalized black.'[21] He sends the Soviets only information dealing with Africa.

The mediators, the double agents, are discovered and undone by the agency of the characters occupying the neutral term, the synthesis of the two negations, the anti-Communist and the colonial, a strange combination that appears in both novels. In le Carré it is the Australian Tarr who brings the news of the mole and sets the hunt going; in Greene, it is the South African intelligence chief Muller whose suspicions of Castle lead to his discovery. These mediators, neither British nor Third World, neither Americans nor Communists, are the darkest shadows in the novels. Though they enable the discovery of the moles, the English characters are very uncomfortable with their presence and their help. So we have a tentative mapping that looks something like this:

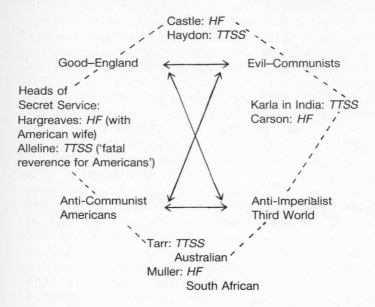

Castle: *HF*
Haydon: *TTSS*

Good–England ⟷ Evil–Communists

Heads of
Secret Service:
Hargreaves: *HF* (with
American wife)
Alleline: *TTSS* ('fatal
reverence for Americans')

Karla in India: *TTSS*
Carson: *HF*

Anti-Communist
Americans

Anti-Imperialist
Third World

Tarr: *TTSS*
Australian
Muller: *HF*
South African

This map is meant as a way of highlighting the structures that these very different novels share; it does not pretend to exhaust their intricacies. However, if one returns to the Philby case itself, one finds that neither of the novelists uses what Philby claims in his autobiography is the true story – that he grew demoralized with the Labour Party and became a Communist. Haydon never mentions Communism; he's simply anti-American in the Cold War. Castle is explicitly not a Communist; 'I've never pretended to share your faith,' he tells the Soviet control, 'I'll never be a Communist.' Furthermore, the journalistic explanations of Philby, the accounts written about him, have often used the same narrative devices as these novels. One version says he was anti-American; and indeed it was largely American secrets that he gave away. Another version says that he was anti-colonialist, that he followed his father, whose respect for Arab culture led him, in his later years, to act out another celebrated English myth: he 'went native.' Even those who accept Philby's account of how he became a Communist have always looked for a missing mediator, the Fourth Man, who is said to have recruited and seduced Burgess, Maclean, and Philby. This narrative impulse in popular ideology is seen in le Carré's own essay on Philby: 'In this most Marxian of novels, where thesis and antithesis are endemic to protagonist, institution and reader alike, it is arguable that even the principal character is still missing. In the lives of Burgess, Maclean and Philby, we discern his hand, his influence, his shadow: never once do we see his face or consciously hear his name. He is the Soviet recruiter.'[22] Even the revelation in 1979 of Anthony Blunt's role in the Philby affair has not eliminated this sense of yet another – once a Third, then a Fourth, now a Fifth Man. One could argue that the facts of the Philby case are less significant than these myths; and furthermore, this myth is not one particular version of the case but a set of narrative explanations, a system of recurring characters.

However, if the most interesting characters are those that unite contraries and mediate between apparently rigid opposites, nevertheless, in this narrative of 'who killed Great Britain?' the seme 'Good-English' is interesting. It seems to be occupied by all those minor characters who are betrayed, the people Smiley visits in their exile: Jim Prideaux, with his 'passionate Englishness'; Connie Sachs, who remembers 'the days before "Empire" became a dirty word'; Jerry Westerby, who will become the 'honourable schoolboy' of le Carré's next novel. In *The Human Factor*, the role is placed primarily on Arthur Davis, the young bureaucrat who would like to be James Bond and is mistakenly killed by his bosses. His name recalls the first great English spy, the amateur smallcraft sailor Arthur Davies, in Erskine Childers's *The Riddle of the Sands* (1903), who foils a German plot to invade England.

What Connie says of Bill Haydon, the golden boy turned mole, is true of these others: 'Trained to Empire, trained to rule the waves. All gone. All taken away.'[23] They are rulers with nothing to rule, servants without a service. And this takes us to a slightly different cover story, one not entirely English.

Safe houses

> The withering away of Britain's international power, and subsequently in the seventies, the demise of the British economy itself, have together destroyed the credibility of the professional ideal. Beyond its intrinsic satisfactions (an internal dynamic of personal advancement) the modern, bureaucratic career lacks any moral justification, and where the moral authority is undermined, 'duty' and 'self-discipline' lack recognizable meaning.
>
> — Andrew Tolson, *The Limits of Masculinity* (1977)

The situation of rulers with nothing to rule, and servants with nothing to serve, transcends post-Empire Britain; it seems a contradiction in white-collar work itself, with its promise of authority and vocation and its failure to provide either. And one of the attractions of the spy thriller is that it is a cover story about work, particularly white-collar work, and its readers invest as much in its narration of bureaucratic power struggles and everyday office routine as in its international intrigue. The audience that makes Greene and le Carré bestsellers is largely made up of men of the Anglo-American professional and managerial class. As Greene himself wrote of *The Human Factor*: 'My ambition after the war was to write a novel of espionage free from the conventional violence, which has not, in spite of James Bond, been a feature of the British Secret Service. I wanted to present the Service unromantically as a way of life, men going daily to their office to earn their pensions, the background much like that of any other profession – whether the bank clerk or the business director – an undangerous routine, and within each character the more important private life.'[24] In the next two sections, I will look at the way these novels narrate the antinomies of professional masculinity – the antinomies of public and private, love and loyalty – and then look at the crisis of professional knowledge in these novels of and about knowledge.

The split between the public and the private is a commonplace of contemporary social analysis. Andrew Tolson puts it well when he writes that 'there is in our society a collective masculine culture of work that makes firm distinctions between "work" and "non-work", "work" and "leisure", or "career" and "family".' The professional is characterized by 'an overriding commitment to work, supported by an idealized image of "home".'[25] Yet the world of the spy novel is precisely one where this split has not been made, where public and private are thoroughly intertwined. Indeed, the different attitudes toward the mole in le Carré and Greene derive from their different evaluation of the demands of public and private. Le Carré's resolution of the split can be seen by looking at two complex triangles in *Tinker, Tailor, Soldier, Spy*, one ostensibly public, the other private.

The first triangle is that among Smiley, Bill Haydon, and Jim Prideaux. Haydon recruited and recommended Prideaux for the Circus; Haydon has betrayed the service, and, in particular, Prideaux, who was wounded in the Czech débâcle; Smiley discovered that Haydon is the mole and revealed him. But this professional triangle is undercut by relations of love and friendship. Haydon and Prideaux were, in one character's innuendo, 'really very close indeed,' and Smiley comes to realize that Prideaux, knowing the Czech mission was intended to reveal the mole, warned Haydon, thereby dooming himself, because of his love for Haydon. Smiley sees the irony of Jim's accusation that he, Smiley, had never seen Bill straight; he now sees Jim's 'willed determination not to remember.'

The other triangle lies among Smiley, Haydon, and Ann. Smiley and Haydon were close friends; Ann had betrayed Smiley with Haydon; Haydon had hurt Ann in some way; Ann had left Haydon. But this 'private' triangle is inverted by the revelation that Haydon had seduced Ann on orders from Karla, the Soviet control. Karla 'reckoned,' Haydon tells Smiley, 'that if I were known to be Ann's lover around the place you wouldn't see me very straight when it came to other things.' Ann, he says, was 'the last illusion of the illusionless man.'[26]

Thus the opposition between private and public is crossed by a second opposition between love and loyalty, an opposition on the surface of the text, continually reflected upon by the characters: it is one of le Carré's 'themes.' But the effect of the interaction of these two oppositions is to sanctify the ideology of the separateness of the public and the private; its truth is proved in the pain and failure which accompanies their intertwining. For love is revealed to be self-delusion, the 'willed determination not to remember.' And this is proper in the private realm – so Smiley returns to Ann at the end, acknowledging that she is 'essentially another man's woman.' But it is not proper in the public realm; the case of Bill Haydon establishes that. Smiley realizes when he proves that Haydon is the mole, that he always knew it: 'he had always known it was Bill. Just as Control had known . . . Just as Connie and Jim had known . . . all of them had tacitly shared that unexpressed half-knowledge which like an illness they hoped would go away if it was never owned to, never diagnosed.' Just, indeed, as the reader knows: this thriller does not work if one requires thrillers to baffle the reader until the very end. For Smiley, like the reader, does not want to own to it even then; he defends Bill to himself: 'was not Bill also betrayed? . . . he saw with painful clarity an ambitious man born to the big canvas, brought up to rule, divide and conquer, whose visions and vanities were fixed, like Percy's, upon the world's game; for whom the reality was a poor island with scarcely a voice that would carry across the water.' Thinking of this man who was 'the torch bearer of a certain kind of antiquated romanticism, a notion of English calling,' Smiley feels 'a surge of resentment against the institution he was supposed to be protecting.' Authority and vocation, the promises of professionalism, are both betrayed.[27]

But there is a difference between betrayal in the home and betrayal at work. So though Smiley returns to Ann, he won't protect Haydon, the way Jim did: 'there's always a part of us that belongs to the public domain,' the Minister had said, 'the social contact cuts both ways.'[28] There is a duty even to an absent service, even to the hollow shell of the Circus Smiley commands at the end.

To parody Lévi-Strauss, one might say that the overrating of love relations in the private sphere justifies the underrating of love relations in the public sphere. And indeed this is at one with le Carré's critique, in his Philby essay, of the Establishment who were blind to and protected Philby. They identified, he writes, 'class with loyalty,' though le Carré's notion of class is closer to caste, Establishment, or better, Ann's 'Set — her word for family and ramifications.'[29] The overrating of kinship ties in the public realm, the lack of separation of private and public, was responsible for the fall.

Graham Greene's novel begins with the separation of public and private. Castle is the archetypal bureaucrat isolating home from work. 'In a bizarre profession anything which belongs to an everyday routine gains great value' and that security and routine is provided by home and family. But the separation is not natural, or real; we discover that Sarah had begun not as his wife but as his agent and that his work-life as a double agent is a consequence of his private life, of his debt to the Communists who helped Sarah escape from South Africa. 'His love of Sarah had led him to Carson [the Communist], and Carson finally to Boris [the Soviet agent]. A man in love walks through the world like an anarchist, carrying a time bomb.' Greene's metaphysic of love is an argument for the priority of the private life over the public, and a lament for its impossibility. For it is Castle's private life, his genuine love for Sarah, that justifies his treason to the reader and to Sarah: she says, 'we have our own country. You and I and Sam. You've never betrayed that country, Maurice.' But it is precisely in asserting the priority of the private that Castle destroys it; he and Sarah are left separated, in Russia and England, with no prospect of reunion.[30]

The subplot of Colonel Daintry, the investigator, repeats this; he is shocked by the illegal, mistaken killing of Davis, so, after doing his duty and reporting that Castle was the leak, he resigns, repudiating his public self. But the service with its secrets has already destroyed his marriage: 'he told himself he was a free man, that he had no duties any longer and no obligations, but he had never felt such an extreme solitude as he felt now.'[31] The public sphere has lost its justification, the private sphere its consolation. *The Human Factor* is a much darker book than le Carré's; for all its occasional sentimentality the despair and isolation of the bureaucrats – Davis, Castle, and Daintry – is convincing.

There is, however, a mediating figure, a utopian space, that appears on the horizon of these cover stories of work and home, a place that can, on occasion, resolve the contradiction between public and private. Smiley thinks that 'at the heart of this plot lay a device so simple that it left him genuinely elated by its symmetry. It even had a physical presence here: here in London, a house . . .' A 'safe house' is the jargon; a redundant phrase within the ideology of professionalism but disquieting insofar as its very redundancy calls it into question: not all houses are safe. It is a recurring figure in spy novels, and it designates a place that is neither office nor home. It often unites the worst of both: 'safe houses I have known, thought Guillam, looking round the gloomy flat. He could write of them the way a commercial traveller could write about hotels: from your five-star hall of mirrors in Belgravia, with Wedgwood pilasters and gilded oak leaves, to this two-room scalphunters' shakedown in Lexham Gardens.' But it is also, for Castle, the place where he can speak freely, and talk of the part of his life hidden from both his fellow workers and from Sarah: 'immediately he felt at home in this strange house which he had never visited before.' It is in the safe house that Smiley works at night, as an amateur, outside the service, uncovering the mole. So though neither Greene nor le Carré is able to reconcile the demands of public and private in his plot – neither story has a happy ending – the safe house provides an imaginary space where the contradictions are suspended, and the public and private temporarily united.[32]

Need to know

> Bureaucracy is a circle no one can leave. Its hierarchy is a
> *hierarchy of information.* The top entrusts the lower circles
> with an insight into details, while the lower circles entrust
> the top with an insight into what is universal, and thus they
> mutually deceive each other . . . The general spirit of bureau-
> cracy is the official *secret* . . .
>
> — Karl Marx

If one way these novels narrate the antinomies of white-
collar, professional work is by attempting to manage the
contradictions between public and private, they also take
on the story of the work itself. But the representation of
work, of a labor process, is a difficult and complex narrative
problem. For the very nature of most work – repetitive,
boring, and partial – makes it difficult to assimilate to a
story. If one thinks of representations of factory work, they
often focus as much on the exceptional cessation of work,
the strike, as on the daily routine itself. A similar issue arises
in representing the 'mental labor' of the office. A man at a
desk processing papers is hardly the material of storytelling.
What gives the storyness to white-collar work, and what
emerges as the subject of the spy novel, are the politics of the
office, the narrative of the hierarchy itself. And since this
hierarchy is, as Marx says, a hierarchy of *information*, these
become stories of information, knowledge, and secrets:
need to know tales. Another way to put this is to say that
these novels foreground, to use Greimas's terms, the cognitive dimension of narrative ('what do I know?') over the
pragmatic dimension ('what happens?').[33] They are closer
to the detective or mystery paradigm, retracing an already
completed action to discover its agency, than to the adventure paradigm, a series of actions united by a hero (the
paradigm that dominates the James Bond stories).

Tinker, Tailor, Soldier, Spy and *The Human Factor* are
both 'need to know' tales; however, they locate themselves
quite differently in the hierarchy of information. Le Carré's
protagonist, George Smiley, is a detective, the hunter;

Greene's protagonist, Castle, is the double agent, the hunted. If we look closely at the role of information in *Tinker, Tailor, Solider, Spy*, we see that Smiley's success comes from accumulating information. At the beginning of the tale he is doubly 'unmanned': he is unemployed and he is cuckolded. By the end, he has regained his career, in a higher position, and he is about to return to his wife (their reconciliation is confirmed at the beginning of *The Honourable Schoolboy*, where they are broken apart again in order to generate another narrative). These resolutions are tentative and partial; the Circus that Smiley heads is barely alive after the discovery of the mole, and his return to Ann is with the acknowledgment of her infidelity. Nevertheless, the partial restitution of Smiley's 'masculinity' is a dividend of his accumulation of information.

Smiley accumulates this information by visiting the betrayed and exiled characters and exchanges his trust and love for their knowledge; this culminates in Smiley's recognition of the mole, as well as of his own and others' complicity. Smiley's knowledge is amateur, humane, and totalizing. He is a scholarly man who studies German Baroque poetry; he has been a don, and the teacher/pupil relationship is seen as an ideal throughout the book, particularly in the Prideaux/ Bill Roach relationship. Smiley collects his information from a position outside the Circus and his profession. He becomes the advocate for the faithful but dismissed servants: Connie, Sam, Max, Jerry, Jim.

But Smiley's knowledge is in service to, and set in opposition to, a very different sort of knowledge: the arcane secrets that are the currency of the spy trade. This knowledge is professional, technical, and fragmentary. It is clearly a relation of power; every reader of spy thrillers knows that the interest is not in the secret information itself – how many missiles, or what secret treaty – but in the distribution of knowledge. Power is knowing what they know without their knowing that you know it. If they know you know, you've lost it. And in fact, if you don't know they know you know it, then they've got the power. And it is that 'simple' relation that is at the heart of many of the spy thrillers of the

le Carré/Greene generation. After Smiley has unraveled all
the knots in Karla's plot, leaving sidekick Guillam 'reeling
with a kind of furious awe,' Smiley says 'the permutations
are infinite, once you've brought off the basic lie.'[34]

This secret knowledge can be seen as a figure for the
experience of knowledge in white-collar work, for the
experienced gap between the 'universality' of a 'liberal'
education, with its knowledge of German Baroque poets,
and the social divisions of mental labor. Nicos Poulantzas,
a marxist theorist of the middle strata, the 'new petty
bourgeoisie,' writes of 'the essential features of the "secrecy
of knowledge" (bureaucratic secrecy) . . . : the various
petty-bourgeois agents each possess, in relation to those
subordinate to them, a fragment of the fantastic secret of
knowledge that legitimates the delegated authority that
they exercise. This is the very meaning of "hierarchy". Each
bureaucratized instance both subordinates and is subordinated; everyone is at the same time both "superior" and
"inferior" to someone else.' One begins to see the sources of
the power of a spy novel convention like the 'need to know'
principle (as Alan Stewart, Desmond Bagley's hero, says of
his superior: 'he worked on the "need to know" principle
and what you didn't know wouldn't hurt him'), as well as
the proliferation of files and dossiers in these books. As
Harry Braverman has written, 'the capitalist mode of production systematically destroys all-around skills where they
exist, and brings into being skills and occupations that
correspond to its needs. Technical capacities are henceforth
distributed on a strict "need to know" basis.'[35]

To return to Smiley: he is on the one hand a throwback to
an earlier notion of knowledge as the possession of an
amateur who uses it to serve the Empire; one thinks of
Arthur Davies's expert but amateur knowledge of small-
craft sailing in *The Riddle of the Sands*. But Smiley is also a
figure for the collective activity of all those disconnected,
alcoholic bureaucrats – Sam, Max, Connie, Jim – whose
fragments of knowledge are unified by Smiley to bring forth
the whole fantastic secret. The discovery of the mole is
theirs, and it is they who are the unnamed killers of Haydon,

though Jim may be the executioner.

If we turn to *The Human Factor*, it is evident that Smiley's role is vacant. There is no totalizing, humane knowledge, just boxes. When Castle goes to the Soviet control, Boris, he is told: 'we live in boxes and it's they who choose the box.' Castle thinks: 'How often he had heard the same comparison in his own office. Each side shares the same clichés.' The boxes are little fragments of knowledge; they must be 'watertight' with no 'leaks.' There are no amateurs in this book. Because of this box-vision, all action occurs in ignorance; even the bosses kill the wrong man. There is a full separation of ends and means. Percival explains this to Daintry (who occupies the Smiley role of investigator), using an abstract painting of squares of different colors as an analogy: 'Percival pointed at a yellow square. "There's your Section 6. That's your square from now on. You don't need to worry about the blue and the red. All you have to do is pinpoint our man and then tell me. You've no responsibility for what happens in the blue or red squares. In fact not even in the yellow. You just report. No bad conscience. No guilt." ' Daintry is left the way Smiley begins, unemployed and alone. As the jargon has it, he is 'out in the cold.'[36]

If we look at all of le Carré's Smiley novels in this way, an interesting narrative and, indeed, ideological development can be seen, one that throws into question the happy ending of *Tinker, Tailor, Soldier, Spy* with its successful totalizing knowledge. For all of them have a similar structure of knowledges: but unlike *The Human Factor* the best figure is not that of discrete squares; rather it might be seen as boxes inside of boxes, a sort of 'Russian doll' like the one used as the emblem of the television production of *Tinker, Tailor, Soldier, Spy*. In each novel, the main characters are finally shown to be unwitting pawns in a game much deeper than the one they think they are involved in. This is the pathos of Leamas in *The Spy Who Came in from the Cold*, who thinks he is after the East German agent Mundt, but is in reality set up to strengthen Mundt's position, since Mundt is a British mole. It is the position of both Leiser and Avery, the anachronistic cold warriors in *The Looking-Glass War*. It is the fate of the Nazi hunter Harting in *A Small Town in Germany*, when cold war politics take precedence over revealing Nazis. And it is also the pathos of Smiley in the second book of the trilogy, *The Honourable Schoolboy*, hung out to dry, as it turns out that the operation he masterminds in Southeast Asia is an unwitting part of an operation of the 'Cousins,' the Americans.

But though the structures are similar, with each new character betrayed by the game, the position of George Smiley changes in an interesting way. In the first two spy novels, Smiley is a relatively minor character who appears as a sort of *deus ex machina*, the figure of the organization betraying its own men. It is he who sets up Leamas in *The Spy Who Came in from the Cold*, and is watching at the Berlin Wall when Leamas and Liz are shot down. It is Smiley who tells Avery near the end of *The Looking-Glass War*: 'We're disowning him [Leiser, the agent in the field, involved in a one-man invasion of East Germany]. It's never a pretty process. He's as good as caught already, don't you see.' To which Avery, who set up the operation, objects: 'You can't do it . . . You can't just leave him there for some squalid diplomatic reason.'[37] But of course they can and do.

In the trilogy of the 1970s, Smiley steps from the shadows to the foreground and becomes a hero, beginning with his success in ferreting out the mole. But at the end of the second book of the Smiley trilogy, *The Honourable Schoolboy*, which takes place largely in Southeast Asia, it is Smiley himself who is left out to dry. As Peter Guillam, Smiley's assistant, thinks: 'he became with every moment more convinced that he was looking at a spider's web, and that only George Smiley, obsessed by the promise of the case and by the image of Karla, was myopic enough, and trusting enough, and in his own paradoxial way innocent enough, to bumble straight into the middle of it.' So behind the similar narrative structures of each book is a kind of narrative across the books, a narrative of ever larger Russian dolls, and of ever smaller and less powerful roles for Smiley. Smiley descends the hierarchy of information from the cold executioner of the Circus, the shadowy figure at the end of the tale who epitomizes absolute bureaucratic knowledge, to the middle-ground hero of *Tinker, Tailor, Soldier, Spy* who embodies a unified knowledge of the fragmented puppets against that of the total organization, and finally, in *The Honourable Schoolboy*, to a puppet himself. As he writes to Ann at the end of *The Honourable Schoolboy*: 'Today, all I know is that I have learned to interpret the whole of life in terms of conspiracy. That is the sword I have lived by, and as I look round me now I see it is the sword I shall die by as well. These people terrify me but I am one of them. If they stab me in the back, then at least that is the judgment of my peers.'[38] Indeed, it seems that the relative failure of the final part of the trilogy, Smiley's triumph over Karla in *Smiley's People*, lies in this intertextual narrative. For after the picture of Smiley caught in the Cousins' web in Southeast Asia, the return to the anachronistic émigré groups and 'cold warriors' in *Smiley's People* shows that the final victory over Karla is not really a victory at all, merely another move in a game of old men. The final scene at the Berlin Wall replays the final scene of *The Spy Who Came in from the Cold*, this time as a 'success,' but hollow and too late.

Thus there is another side to the popular story of Smiley as hero, the successful narrative of white-collar heroics in the Cold War; it is the deeper, more critical tale where the real enemy is the organization itself, the organization that never keeps faith, the organization that betrays its own men. This was the heart of Len Deighton's *The Ipcress File*, a tale where the mole is neither one's friend and colleague (like Smiley's Haydon) nor the protagonist himself (like Castle), but one's bureaucratic superior. This story has been recently reworked in Robert McCrum's *In the Secret State* (1980), a novel that can be set against le Carré's unsuccessful 1979 resurrection of the heroic Smiley in the Cold War plots of *Smiley's People*. Here there is no mole at all; the information leaking from the C Directorate is not going to the 'other side' but is being sold to multinationals and private data collecting businesses. As Frank Strange, the loyal servant, says, summing up his investigation on a tape recording played after his death:

There are no agents. The system was never penetrated from the outside. I'm forced to the conclusion that no one cares about us enough to bother with that any-more. No, the answer is sadder and more disgraceful. We are corrupting ourselves from within. That's where the enemy is, burrowing from the inside, almost invis-ibly.[39]

McCrum's tale uses the 'need to know' formulas of le Carré, Greene, and Deighton to narrate a world of private compu-ter databases and the illicit surveillance of ordinary citizens, of covert alliances between governments and multinational corporations, and of the Official Secrets Act. Whereas the novels of le Carré increasingly serve as a romantic cover story for the security services (as E.P. Thompson notes, 'many people have only the haziest notion as to the character and functions of MI5, MI6 or the Special Branch of the police . . . they are thought of as . . . counter-espionage agencies playing a John le Carré game of spooks with the Russians'[40]), McCrum takes the story of the spy betrayed by his own organization to reconstruct the thriller of the 'secret service' as a thriller of the 'secret state.'

Conclusion

In 1972, Julian Symons surveyed the history of the spy novel and concluded that it had reached a point of exhaustion: 'After the varied talents of Fleming, le Carré, and Deighton, it is difficult to see how the spy story can go much further at present, although perhaps it can be absorbed into a novel or be used as the basis for a new kind of documentary approach. . . . It would be in everybody's long term interest if a moratorium could be declared on the writing of spy stories for the next ten years.'[1] More than a decade later the moratorium is still not in sight. The spy thriller remains a popular and active genre and continues to provide cover stories of technical and professional work and of national and imperial ideologies. Why does the spy have such resonance in twentieth-century Anglo-American culture? Why is the genre of the thriller the site of imaginative struggles between formulas with very different political and ideological accents? I want to try to answer these questions in this conclusion by looking briefly at three directions the spy thriller has taken in the last decade: the fate of the thriller of the 'mole,' the development of the documentary thriller of 'secret histories,' and the emergence of left-wing thrillers of the near future.

The spy novel of moles and rival services that le Carré and Deighton pioneered continues to be written and to find readers, despite Symons's predictions. It is arguable that le

Carré's own work of the 1970s, the Smiley trilogy, is his finest. And a number of other adepts of the Circus have appeared – one thinks of Joseph Hone, Paul Henissart, W.T. Tyler, Robert McCrum, and Gavin Lyall (of the Major Maxim series). Though there is a sense of exhaustion in the increasingly formulaic double agents and triple crosses, and though none of these writers has captured an audience outside of the genre, Bill Haydon's comment in *Tinker, Tailor, Soldier, Spy* that the 'secret services were the only real measure of a nation's political health, the only real expression of its subconscious,' and le Carré's statement, in his own voice, that the secret services are 'microcosms of the British condition, of our social attitudes and vanities,' seem to win a deep consent among readers of various political camps.[2] The range and limits of the 'mole' formula can be seen in two of le Carré's most ambitious novels, *The Honourable Schoolboy* and *The Little Drummer Girl*. *The Honourable Schoolboy* attempts to use the microcosm of the secret service to tell the story of Southeast Asia, taking the genre beyond the limits of Cold War Europe; however, its success is not as a novel of Vietnam (where it labors under the influence of earlier Third World plots of Conrad and Graham Greene) but as a cover story of the relations between Britain and the 'Cousins,' the United States. Indeed, British espionage formulas have seemed a particularly appropriate cover story for the cracks in American world hegemony after Vietnam; thus one finds American writers like Robert Littell and Charles McCarry adopting the spy thriller in the 1970s and 1980s. The Vietnam War may come to stand to the American spy thriller as the South African War stood to the British spy thriller, inaugurating a line of cover stories of empire lost.

Le Carré's *The Little Drummer Girl*, on the other hand, marks the clear limits of this formula. The attempt to narrate the struggle of the Palestinians against Israel through the plots of Cold War secret services is confused and unconvincing. The strongest parts of the novel are the scenes set in Germany, where le Carré's sense of place does not betray him; the scenes that take place in the Middle East read like tourist notes. The reviewers' controversy over le Carré's political stance can be easily resolved if one considers the opposition he depicts between the Israelis and the Palestinians in the light of that between the English and the East Germans in his previous novels: for le Carré, the Israelis, like the English, are 'our' side, corrupt, duplicitous, and not particularly admirable; the Palestinians, like the East Germans, are the 'other' side who turn out to be nobler and more human than was thought possible. But this narrative translation does not work; the manipulations of the English actress Charlie by both sides seem to mirror le Carré's own lack of control.

The most successful recent tale of moles, Julian Rathbone's *A Spy of the Old School* (1982), reinforces the sense that this formula is tied to a particular world in a particular period. For unlike Greene and le Carré, who set their meditations on Philby in the present, Rathbone manages to sum up the genre by writing what is essentially a historical novel. It is true that the investigation and eventual killing of the mole, Richard Austen, is set in the present of 1980; nonetheless, the heart of the book lies in the history that precedes the newspaper of 1955 which Austen finds in the opening scene. The life of Richard Austen has all the layers that have made this cover story so powerful: the petty tyrannies and sexual confusion of the public school; the attraction of the intellectual Left at Cambridge; the experience of the Spanish Civil War and the discovery of the fascist sympathies of the British elite; the wartime intelligence work at Bletchley Park; and the 'atom bomb spies' and 'missing diplomats' of the Cold War. And it is reconstructed from a number of texts: Austen's autobiography; the files consulted by the investigator, Cargill; the research of an academic; the uncertain memories of participants; and a skeleton found on a building site. But the success of the novel comes from its depiction of Austen as archaeologist; the details of archaeology underlie the narrative's events and its explanation systems. So Austen's meeting with Philby in Turkey in 1948, a virtuoso scene, is cast not in the tourist mode of Bond in Istanbul, but in the context of

Austen's first professional dig. Austen's childhood discovery of the starkness of the class boundary between gentry and laborer, between intellectual and manual work, takes place on his first dig, providing the link between Austen's 'twin obsessions' – archaeology and socialism. The archaeological material also makes Austen's marxism, inflected by the work of V. Gordon Childe, more convincing than that of any previous fictional mole. And Austen's directorship of the Gold Museum is a fitting emblem of his position, caught between the corporate support of his cousin Slaker and his marxist understanding of the Bronze Age. Rathbone's marxist archaeologist is a descendant of Ambler's alliance of the Soviet spy and the English engineer as well as the moles of le Carré and Greene. But this history ends in the death of both investigator and spy. Both attempt to break from their superiors in order to remain faithful to their original commitments; and both are sacrificed to the corporate interests of the Slaker Group. Rathbone's tale serves not only as the finest history of the spies of the old school but as their epitaph.

Rathbone's historical concerns link him to the second path that the thriller has taken in the last decade, a path which has captured a mass international audience. As if following Symons's advice, using the spy story as the 'basis for a new kind of documentary approach,' a number of writers have produced bestselling documentary thrillers. The best-known are those of Frederick Forsyth and Ken Follett, though the recent novels of Len Deighton are in this line as well. In retrospect, Forsyth's *The Day of the Jackal* (1971) seems as much of a departure for the thriller as *Ashenden, Casino Royale* or *The Ipcress File*. One critic has gone so far as to argue that *The Day of the Jackal* is not a thriller; but it would seem more accurate to say that it changed the formula of the thriller.[3]

This new formula might be called the 'secret history,' as it distinguishes itself from earlier thrillers by crossing the spy thriller with the masculine adventure story (represented earlier by such writers as Alistair MacLean and Hammond Innes) and the historical novel. These new thrillers create elaborately documented historical narratives on the basis of a counterfactual premise (for example, that the Nazis occupied Britain in Deighton's *SS-GB*) or an invented, but apparently non-falsifiable, history that can be sewn into the fabric of documented history (for example, the account of the German spy in England in World War II in Follett's *Eye of the Needle*). The premise is, as Follett puts it in the preface to *Eye of the Needle*: 'That much is history. What follows is fiction. Still and all, one suspects something like this must have happened.'

One of the central pleasures of these texts is the extreme concern for detail regarding things, places, and dates. We know that *The Day of the Jackal* opens at 6:40 a.m. on 11 March 1963 and ends on 25 August 1963. If, in the passage from Ambler's *Journey into Fear* discussed above (p. 76), we are told that a gun had stamped on it the name of an American typewriter manufacturer, in the thrillers of Forsyth we are told the name of the manufacturer and probably the catalog number of the weapon as well. This intensification of the 'reality effect,' the assertion of verisimilitude through the amassing of convincing and verifiable details of everyday life, is called forth not only by the 'historical' claims of the narrative, but by a new interest in the information gathering aspect of espionage at the expense of the Great Game of double agents.

A second aspect of these thrillers is the fetishization of professionalism. The protagonists are consummate professionals, to the point of having no affective life whatsoever. The antinomy between the public and the private is 'resolved' by characters whose being denies any private life, though this leads inevitably to their destruction. The Jackal, the Needle, Wolff (in Follett's *The Key to Rebecca*): these protagonists are mercenaries who mobilize the reader's sympathies simply by their position in the foreground, even though they are working for the 'wrong' side. These thrillers are usually constructed as two simultaneous stories, and switch back and forth from the narrative of the mercenary's plan to the narrative of the hunt for him. As the two stories get closer and closer together, the suspense builds, even though the reader knows the outcome all along – that, for example, de Gaulle was not assassinated and that Rommel did not take Cairo.

One of the most convincing explanations for the popularity of these 'secret histories' is offered by John Sutherland, who argues that they are inspired by 'the ineradicable popular belief that the *real* facts of history are never given.'[4] And many of these thrillers – including Follett's *Eye of the Needle* and *The Key to Rebecca*, Forsyth's *The Odessa File*, Deighton's *SS-GB*, and Jack Higgins's *The Eagle Has Landed* – tell the secret history of the Second World War, reaching back to the origins of the Cold War Europe of Fleming, le Carré, and the early Deighton. Sutherland's explanation for this – that the thirty years required for declassifying government documents had passed – is not fully convincing. Rather these thrillers are a significant part of a continuing struggle over the popular memory of the war. The historian E.P. Thompson has written:

> One is not permitted to speak of one's wartime reminiscences today, nor is one under any impulse to do so . . . It is so, in part, because Chapman Pincher and his like have made an uncontested takeover of all the moral assets of that period; have coined the war into Hollywood blockbusters and spooky paperbacks and television tedia; have attributed all the values of that moment to the mythic virtues of an authoritarian Right which is now, supposedly, the proper inheritor and guardian of the present nation's interests . . . My memories of that war are very different. I recall a resolute and ingenious civilian army, increasingly hostile to the conventional military virtues, which became – far more than any of my younger friends will begin to credit – an anti-fascist and consciously anti-imperialist army. Its members voted Labour in 1945: knowing why, as did the civilian workers at home.[5]

Thompson accurately notes the role of popular fiction in shaping the ideological legacy of the war. However, an attention to the 'secret history' thrillers indicates that that legacy is shifting, that the adventure formulas of wartime heroics are no longer convincing, no longer adequate. The economic crisis of the 1970s, the end of the post-war boom, led to a new vision of the meaning and results of the war. Not only has this vision displaced the memory of the heroic founding of a new, social democratic society, but it has also begun to displace the popular conservative tales of war heroism that made Alistair MacLean a longterm bestseller, eventually outselling even Ian Fleming.[6] For these 'secret histories' are haunted by the sense that the war was really lost, that the West German 'economic miracle' was not matched by a British 'miracle.' Just as the spy thriller began as the compensatory myth of the crisis of imperialism, so these 'historical' thrillers of German spies serve as compensatory tales of post-war decline, telling the *real* origins of the present crisis.[7] However, their cover stories are contradictory: while their mercenary protagonists demonstrate the failures of a tradition of the amateur, they are finally defeated by British resistance. For all their anxious replaying of history as it might have been, their endings are rescued by history as it was – the Germans were defeated.

The third direction the thriller has taken in the last decade has not had the popular success of the secret histories of Follett and Forsyth, but it is significant for those concerned with the politics of popular culture. In his 1940 essay on 'Boys' Weeklies,' George Orwell noted that 'in England, popular imaginative literature is a field that left-wing thought has never begun to enter.'[8] Almost half a century later, Orwell's comment remains largely accurate, even though the manifest politics of the thriller and its popular audience make it a genre particularly appropriate for socialist fiction. Despite the tradition of thrillers critical of the social order, from those of Ambler, Greene, and le Carré to recent ones by Robert McCrum and Julian Rathbone, the thriller remains dominated by the politics of the right, whether in the survivals of imperial and Cold War mentalities or in the dominance of racist and sexist codes. However, in the last decade there has been a modest development of the socialist thriller, and, in the final section of this conclusion, I will look briefly at three of them: Ivan Ruff's *The Dark Red Star* (1985); Chris Mullin's *A Very British Coup* (1982); and Raymond Williams's *The Volunteers* (1978).[9]

Despite some striking differences, they all share a formula which has not been important in the spy thriller since the time of Le Queux and Oppenheim: they are all set in the near future. The war prophecy tales of Le Queux, like his *The Invasion of 1910* (published in 1906), were usually set several years in the future so as to tell of the fulfillment of a present threat. And E. Phillips Oppenheim often set his fantasies of royalist restorations in the near future: *Gabriel Samara* (1925) has the Bolsheviks overthrown and the Czar restored. Ruff, Mullin, and Williams all turn to these un-likely reactionary precursors in order to explore contradictions and possibilities that remain latent in the present, and to narrate scenarios and strategies in a context that is neither utopian nor limited by the actual and immediate. So Williams's novel of 1978 is set in 1987, Mullin's novel of 1982 in 1989, and Ruff's novel of 1985 in 1990; however, each depicts a different future.

Ivan Ruff's *The Dark Red Star* is of interest because it was the first spy thriller in a series of left-wing crime novels published by the socialist press Pluto, a series which marked one of the first substantial left entries into the field of popular fiction. It is a competent thriller which replays the formula of the mole. A ghost-writer for celebrities gets involved in writing the biography of an ex-Tory Prime Minister, a figure of the extreme right, and discovers that the former Prime Minister has been a Soviet mole through-out his career, aided by a celebrated Russian dissident and émigré. It is a fairly simple reversal of the earlier tales of moles, a 'great impersonation' which brands the far right as traitors.

Chris Mullin's *A Very British Coup* also turns the narrative of treason and betrayal around, but in a much more successful way. In this near future, a radical Labour government is elected, to the consternation of the civil service, the press barons, and particularly the secret services. The novel consists of three successive confrontations between the government of Harry Perkins and the British Establishment: a bank crisis, a power workers' strike provoked by a right-wing labor leader, and an attempt to expel American bases from Britain. The secret service takes the lead in undermining the government, in a 'very British' version of the fate of Allende in Chile: a bloodless coup succeeds through a somewhat hackneyed sex scandal. But the interest and power of this thriller comes as the British secret service allies with the Americans to subvert the British government; the nationalist tale of betrayal is mobilized against the fellow travelers of the American empire. Giving a new accent to the 'Cousins,' Mullin manages to shift the world system of the thriller when the Labour Prime Minister asks the defense establishment: 'What I'd like to know . . . is against whom are we defending ourselves?'[10]

In the most interesting of these thrillers, Raymond Williams leaves the world of MI5 and MI6, writing a thriller that recalls Eric Ambler's tales of innocents caught in secret worlds of political intrigue. *The Volunteers* is the story of Lewis Redfern, a reporter who covers the political underground for a multinational news service in a time, 1987, when a coalition government rules a partially devolved Britain. The investigation of an attempted assassination of a Cabinet Minister in Wales leads Redfern to untangle a web spun by two sets of 'spies': the government agents in the underground and the 'Volunteers,' an organization which infiltrates the Establishment, the corporations and the state with 'sleepers,' secret radicals. Like Ambler, Williams centers on the dilemma of the 'innocent' technician, as Redfern finds himself in a situation where the line between observer and participant, reporter and informer, is hard to distinguish. Caught between his employers, the underground, and the Welsh mining community, he 'volunteers,' giving up his job and testifying for the miners; nevertheless, he ends up alone and cut off from everyone.

When Williams was asked whether he was deliberately using the form of the thriller for political purposes when he wrote *The Volunteers*, he replied:

No. It was always much more an option for a convention that would allow me to write my material than a decision to use a convention to get a different kind of reader. When I got sent the jacket of the book and saw it described as a political thriller, I was surprised. But when I said so to the publisher, he replied: 'Years ago, you remarked to me that it would be perfectly possible to take a popular format like the thriller and put it to good use.' So who knows?[11]

However, the adoption of the thriller conventions has significant effects on the novel. Despite Williams's and Redfern's insistence that the heart of the story is the death of a striking miner, the working-class novel of Welsh miners within *The Volunteers* (which finds its voice in the interpolated pamphlet of the Gwent Writer's Group, *Death of a Loader*) is eventually subordinated to the intrigues of the shadow world of spies and the dilemmas of the reporter Redfern. Like the thrillers of Ambler, le Carré, and Deighton, it is a tale of the political contradictions of white-collar, professional work. But unlike Ambler, who revealed the political implications of the work his engineers thought entirely apolitical, or the novelists of the secret services, who depict the dangers of office routines in organizations that betray their own people, Williams projects an imaginary future to explore the political strategies of radicals within the professional and managerial classes, of 'volunteers' in the offices of the media, the state, and the corporations.

The appeal of Williams's thriller transcends the political strategies it narrates, which range from the flamboyant terrorism of the assassin to the secret Fabianism of the 'Volunteers.' Rather it lies in his representing the dilemmas of meaningful public action while at the same time imagining its possibility. Indeed, this is a central appeal of the spy thriller, the tale of secret agents; it serves as a way of narrating individual political agency in a world of institutions and states that seem to block all action and paralyze all opposition. In its two main traditions, the thriller redeems the worlds of white-collar work and consumerist leisure: in the thriller of work, the anxieties of the organization man take on a secret coherence, and bureaucratic routines are invested with political meaning; in the thriller of leisure, the sports and games that kill time become a killing time, a time of dangerous political contests. Of the genres of popular fiction, only science fiction takes stories of public, political life as seriously as the thriller, and in science fiction they are displaced to other worlds. The crime novel primarily investigates the murders of the private sphere, the horror novel tells of the uncanny in psychic life, and romantic fiction is divided between the perils of courtship and the sagas of family dynasties. Le Carré's George Smiley thinks at one point that 'It is sheer vanity to believe that one fat middle-aged spy is the only person capable of holding the world together'; but from Richard Hannay on, that is the premise of the thriller.[12]

The other major appeal of the spy thriller is its map of the world. Like the romances set in foreign lands and the popular travel books, the thriller takes the globe as its setting; unlike them, its map shows not simply the 'exotic,' but an entire world system, an international order of nations. This map was drawn with the hand of Empire, since the thriller of espionage emerged as an end-of-Empire genre, telling how 'we' were betrayed, not beaten. But its boundaries and relations have been redrawn by subsequent writers, and the thriller remains one of the few genres, popular or literary, that are able to tell an international plot. If these plots often provide mystified and mendacious maps to the international order, it is perhaps less the fault of the genre than of the culture and society which can only imagine the relations between nations and peoples through the conspiracies of secret agents and spies. For a genre is finally a cover story for a culture, and in this lies the success and failure of the spy thriller, its utopia and its ideology.

The thriller has produced cover stories for the cultures of imperialist nations, stories which have, as George Smiley said, paralleled that imperial reality, expressing the identities and appetites they attempt to conceal, attempting to resolve in the imaginary world of secret services the contradictory processes of the world system – two world wars, the revolutions of 1917 and after, the anti-colonial struggles of Asia and Africa, the rivalries of capitalist states, and the Cold War between the superpowers. The ability to provide persuasive and sometimes illuminating narratives to cover these world-historical events and processes has given the spy thriller its power, range, and importance; one doubts that any 'moratorium' on the writing of spy stories is likely to occur without significant social change in the first world: spies are central to our collective cover stories. However, the translation of the world into the shadow world of spies is finally a somewhat impoverished and impoverishing figure, however powerful. Graham Greene caught both the ideological and the utopian moment of the figure in his spy novel, *The Human Factor*:[13] at one point, the mole Castle begins telling his son Sam about the imaginary dragon he had as a child. The dragon lived on the Common: 'I knew I had only to give a signal,' he tells Sam, 'and [the dragon] would leave his dugout on the Common and come down and help me. We had a lot of private signals, codes, ciphers . . .

' "Like a spy," Sam said.

' "Yes," Castle said with disappointment, "I suppose so. Like a spy." '[13]

Like Castle we are disappointed with the simile; but we return again to our cover stories of spies and secret agents.

Notes

1 Thrillers, shockers, spy novels

1 Eric Ambler (ed.), *To Catch a Spy* (London: Fontana, 1974), 19.
2 Guy Bouchard, 'Le roman d'espionage,' *Etudes Littéraires* 7 (1974):23–60.
3 Fredric Jameson, *The Political Unconscious* (Ithaca: Cornell University Press, 1981), 105; 'Magical Narratives: Romance as Genre,' *New Literary History* 7 (1975):157.
4 Here John Cawelti's distinction between the terms 'genre' and 'formula' is useful. Cawelti sees a popular fiction formula as a combination or synthesis of a number of specific cultural conventions with a more universal story form or archetype. A genre, Cawelti argues, is when a formula comes to be looked at by its creators and audiences as a distinctive literary class with certain artistic potentials and limitations. A genre, he says, is a formula looked at aesthetically. I would amend this slightly to say that a genre is a class of narratives whose producers and audience recognize it self-consciously as such, whether that recognition is aesthetic or commercial. A particular genre, say science fiction, may incorporate a number of different formulas. John Cawelti, *Adventure, Mystery, and Romance: Formula Stories as Art and Popular Culture* (Chicago: University of Chicago Press, 1976), 6.
5 See Anthony Boucher, 'Trojan Horse Opera,' and James Sandoe, 'Dagger of the Mind,' in H. Haycraft (ed.), *The Art of the Mystery Story* (New York: Simon & Schuster, 1946); David Skene Melvin, 'The Secret Eye,' *Pacific Moana Quarterly* 3 (January 1978):11–26; and Julian Symons, *Bloody Murder* (Harmondsworth: Penguin, 1974).

6   See Ralph Harper, *The World of the Thriller* (Baltimore: Johns Hopkins University Press, 1974); Bruce Merry, *Anatomy of the Spy Thriller* (London: Gill & Macmillan, 1977); G.J. Rausch and D.K. Rausch, 'Developments in Espionage Fiction,' *Kansas Quarterly* 10 (Fall 1978):71–82; Melvin, 'The Secret Eye.'

7   Tzvetan Todorov, *The Poetics of Prose* (Ithaca: Cornell University Press, 1977).

8   This term is developed in the work of Roger Bromley. See Roger Bromley, 'Natural Boundaries: The Social Function of Popular Fiction,' *Red Letters*, no.7 (1978):34–60; English Studies Group, 'Recent Developments in English Studies at the Centre,' in S. Hall and others, *Culture, Language, Media* (London: Hutchinson, 1980).

9   Symons, *Bloody Murder*, 242.

10 The term signifies the basic unit of the 'essentially antagonistic collective discourses of social classes ... The ideologeme is an amphibious formation, whose essential structural characteristic may be described as its possibility to manifest itself either as a pseudo-idea – a conceptual or belief system, an abstract value, an opinion or prejudice, or as a protonarrative, a kind of ultimate class fantasy about the "collective characters" which are the classes in opposition.' Jameson, *The Political Unconscious*, 87.

11 Warner Berthoff, *The Ferment of Realism* (Cambridge: Cambridge University Press, 1981), xi, xix.

12 Jameson, *The Political Unconscious*, 11.

13 See Ambler, *To Catch a Spy*; Boucher, 'Trojan Horse Opera'; Michael Gilbert, 'The Spy in Fact and Fiction,' in J. Ball (ed.), *The Mystery Story* (Harmondsworth: Penguin, 1978); Rausch and Rausch, 'New Developments'; Sandoe, 'Dagger of the Mind'; Melvin, 'The Secret Eye'; and Symons, *Bloody Murder*. A book-length version of this sequence that adds a number of the minor peaks but remains a series of brief summaries of an author and his or her work is LeRoy Panek, *The Special Branch* (Bowling Green, Ohio: Bowling Green University Popular Press, 1981).

14 See Richard Altick, *The English Common Reader* (Chicago: University of Chicago Press, 1957); Robert Escarpit, *The Sociology of Literature* (London: Frank Cass, 1971); Peter Mann and Jacqueline Burgoyne, *Books and Reading* (London: André Deutsch, 1969); Peter Mann, *Books: Buyers and Borrowers* (London: André Deutsch, 1971).

15 See Cawelti, *Adventure, Mystery, and Romance*; Harper, *The World of the Thriller*; and Merry, *Anatomy of the Spy Thriller*. Jerry Palmer's *Thrillers: Genesis and Structure of a Popular Genre*

(London: Edward Arnold, 1978) is the best of the books on the thriller; however, its strongest section deals with the two major thriller writers of the Cold War, Ian Fleming and Mickey Spillane, and he often generalizes from them to all thrillers.

16 See Q.D. Leavis, *Fiction and the Reading Public* (Harmondsworth: Penguin, 1979); Louis James, *Fiction for the Working Man: 1830—1850* (Harmondsworth: Penguin, 1974); Louis James, *English Popular Literature* (New York: Columbia University Press, 1976); John Sutherland, *Fiction and the Fiction Industry* (London: Athlone Press, 1978); John Sutherland, *Bestsellers* (London: Routledge & Kegan Paul, 1981); English Studies Group, 'Thinking the Thirties,' in F. Barker and others, *1936: The Sociology of Literature, Volume Two* (Colchester: University of Essex, 1979); English Studies Group, 'Recent Developments.'

17 Sutherland, *Fiction*; Sutherland, *Bestsellers*.

18 Graham Greene, *Collected Essays* (Harmondsworth: Penguin, 1970), 171; William Vivian Butler, *The Durable Desperadoes* (London: Macmillan, 1973), 67; John Attenborough, *A Living Memory: Hodder and Stoughton Publishers, 1868—1975* (London: Hodder & Stoughton), 98.

19 Graham Greene, *Ways of Escape* (New York: Pocket Books, 1980), 16.

20 Sutherland, *Fiction*, 176.

21 Nicholas Blake, 'The Detective Story – Why?', in H. Haycraft (ed.), *The Art of the Mystery Story* (New York: Simon & Schuster, 1946), 401; Leavis, *Fiction and the Reading Public*.

22 Ambler, *To Catch a Spy*, 15; Boucher, 'Trojan Horse Opera,' 246; Donald McCormick, *Who's Who in Spy Fiction* (London: Sphere Books, 1979), 18–23.

23 Merry, *Anatomy of the Spy Thriller*, 1.

24 Georg Lukács, *Writer and Critic* (New York: Grosset & Dunlap, 1971), 130, 132, 136.

25 Graham Greene, *Collected Essays*, 172.

26 See Bromley, 'Natural Boundaries'; Gil Davies, 'Teaching about Narrative,' *Screen Education*, no.29 (Winter 1978/1979):56–76.

27 Terry Eagleton, 'Realism and Popular Culture,' *Popular Culture Bulletin, No. 4* (Milton Keynes: Open University, October 1978), 10.

28 Martin Green, *Dreams of Adventure, Deeds of Empire* (New York: Basic Books, 1979).

29 Patrick Howarth, *Play Up and Play the Game: The Heroes of Popular Fiction* (London: Eyre Methuen, 1973).

2 **Sport in a land flowing with strikes and profiteers**
1 Stuart Hall, 'Notes on Deconstructing "the Popular",' in R. Samuel (ed.), *People's History and Socialist Theory* (London: Routledge & Kegan Paul, 1981), 229.
2 Martin Green, *Dreams of Adventure, Deeds of Empire* (New York: Basic Books, 1979), 3, 322–3, 320.
3 Basil Hogarth, *Writing Thrillers for Profit: A Practical Guide* (London: A. & C. Black, 1936).
4 See I.F. Clarke, *Voices Prophesying War 1763—1984* (London: Oxford University Press, 1966); Patrick Dunae, 'Boy's Literature and the Idea of Empire,' *Victorian Studies* 24 (Autumn 1980):105–22.
5 David French, 'Spy Fever in Britain, 1900–1915,' *Historical Journal* 21 (1978):357.
6 See Michael Blanch, 'Imperialism, Nationalism, and Organized Youth,' in John Clarke and others, *Working Class Culture* (London: Hutchinson, 1979), 119; Gareth Stedman Jones, *Languages of Class* (Cambridge: Cambridge University Press, 1983), 181; Robert Roberts, *The Classic Slum* (Harmondsworth: Penguin, 1973), 181; Richard Price, *An Imperial War and the British Working Class* (London: Routledge & Kegan Paul, 1972); Hugh Cunningham, 'The Language of Patriotism, 1750–1914,' *History Workshop Journal*, no.12 (Autumn 1981):8–33.
7 Eric Ambler (ed.), *To Catch a Spy* (London: Fontana, 1974), 15.
8 John Buchan, *The Thirty-Nine Steps* in *The Four Adventures of Richard Hannay* (London: Hodder & Stoughton, 1930), 119–20.
9 Julian Symons, *Bloody Murder* (Harmondsworth: Penguin, 1974), 236.
10 Erskine Childers, *The Riddle of the Sands* (Harmondsworth: Penguin, 1978), 103.
11 Graham Greene, *Collected Essays* (Harmondsworth: Penguin, 1970), 167.
12 E. Phillips Oppenheim, *The Great Impersonation* (Boston: Little, Brown, 1920), 76.
13 Buchan, *The Thirty-Nine Steps*, 99.
14 LeRoy Panek, *Watteau's Shepherds: The Detective Novel in Britain, 1914—1940* (Bowling Green, Ohio: Bowling Green University Popular Press, 1979), 12.
15 Colin Watson, *Snobbery With Violence* (London: Eyre & Spottiswoode, 1971).
16 'Sapper' [H.C. McNeile], *Bull-dog Drummond* (London: Hodder & Stoughton, n.d.), 25, 26, 104–5.
17 'Sapper,' *Bull-dog Drummond*, 312, 122.

18   Hall, 'Notes on Deconstructing, "the Popular",' 233.
19   See Tom Nairn's reflections on nationalism in *The Break-Up of Britain* (London: Verso, 1981).
20   Edgar Wallace, *The Four Just Men* (Harmondsworth: Penguin, 1936), 21.
21   William Vivian Butler, *The Durable Desperadoes* (London: Macmillan, 1973), 53–7.
22   Butler, *The Durable Desperadoes*, 71–2.

3   **Epitaph for an amateur**
 1   Anthony Boucher, 'Trojan Horse Opera,' 246, and James Sandoe, 'Dagger of the Mind,' 260, in H. Haycraft (ed.), *The Art of the Mystery Story* (New York: Simon & Schuster, 1946).
 2   Graham Greene, *Ways of Escape* (New York: Pocket Books, 1980), 54–5.
 3   Graham Greene, *The Ministry of Fear* (Harmondsworth: Penguin, 1975), 65.
 4   English Studies Group, 'Thinking the Thirties,' in F. Barker and others, *1936: The Sociology of Litrature, Volume 2* (Colchester: University of Essex, 1979).
 5   Joel Hopkins, 'An Interview with Eric Ambler,' *Journal of Popular Culture* 9 (Fall 1975):286.
 6   George Orwell, 'Boys' Weeklies,' in *A Collection of Essays* (Garden City, NY: Anchor Books, 1954), 302.
 7   Robert Graves and Alan Hodge, *The Long Weekend: A Social History of Great Britain 1918—1939* (New York: W.W. Norton, 1963), 301.
 8   George Orwell, 'Raffles and Miss Blandish,' in *A Collection of Essays* (Garden City, NY: Anchor Books, 1954), 152–3.
 9   Eric Ambler, *The Dark Frontier* (London: Fontana, 1966), 29, 104–5, 124, 23.
10   Eric Ambler, *The Mask of Dimitrios* (London: Fontana, 1966), 87.
11   Chandler, quoted in Gavin Lambert, *The Dangerous Edge* (New York: Grossman Publishers, 1976), xi; Eric Ambler, *Journey into Fear* (London: Fontana, 1966), 51.
12   Hopkins, 'Interview with Ambler,' 288; Eric Ambler, *Uncommon Danger* (London: Hodder & Stoughton, 1952), 76, 84.
13   Fredric Jameson, 'Class and Allegory in Contemporary Mass Culture: *Dog Day Afternoon* as a Political Film,' *Screen Education*, no.30 (Spring 1979):77, 90.
14   Ambler, *The Mask of Dimitrios*, 20.
15   Ambler, *The Mask of Dimitrios*, 20.
16   Eric Ambler, *Cause for Alarm* (London: Coronet Books, 1973), 38.

17 Ambler, *Cause for Alarm*, 148.

18 Ambler, *Cause for Alarm*, 140, 125; Ambler, *Journey into Fear*, 92.

19 See Gary Werskey, *The Visible College: The Collective Biography of British Scientific Socialists of the 1930s* (New York: Holt, Rinehart & Winston, 1979).

20 Jean-Paul Sartre, *What is Literature?* (New York: Harper & Row, 1965), 134; Ambler, *Cause for Alarm*, 10.

21 Perhaps a brief note on the nature of the American-British connection in popular fiction is in order here. Throughout this book I note particularly the influence of the American hardboiled crime story, developed in the late 1920s and 1930s in the pulp magazines and reaching its most celebrated form in the tales of Dashiell Hammett, Raymond Chandler, and Mickey Spillane, on the British thriller. This is not merely a matter of literary influence or American chauvinism. Rather it is part of an important 'Americanization' of British popular culture through the twentieth century, a process noted (and deplored) by George Orwell and Richard Hoggart, among others. See Ken Worpole, *Dockers and Detectives* (London: Verso, 1983), for a more positive assessment of the 'American connection.' Influences in the other direction are less marked in popular culture than in the American middlebrow Anglophilia, the common equation of 'cultured' with 'English.' An exception is the influence of the British spy novel of le Carré and others on the emergence of American spy novels in the post-Vietnam War 1970s.

22 Ambler, *The Mask of Dimitrios*, 44.

23 Roland Barthes, *S/Z* (New York: Hill & Wang, 1974), 19.

24 Ralph Harper, *The World of the Thriller* (Baltimore: Johns Hopkins University Press, 1974), 75.

25 W. Somerset Maugham, *Ashenden: The British Agent* (New York: Avon Books, 1943), 81, 15.

26 Maugham, *Ashenden*, 7, 187, 213.

27 Maugham, *Ashenden*, 204–5.

28 Ambler, *The Dark Frontier*, 163.

29 Ambler, *Cause for Alarm*, 244.

30 V. Propp, *Morphology of the Folktale* (Austin: University of Texas Press, 1968); Fredric Jameson, *The Prison-House of Language* (Princeton: Princeton University Press, 1972), 67–8.

31 Robert Harling, *The Enormous Shadow* (New York: Harper & Row, 1955), 96.

32 E.P. Thompson, 'Outside the Whale,' in *The Poverty of Theory* (New York: Monthly Review Press, 1978), 229.

33 Ambler, *Journey into Fear*, 191.

34 Graham Greene, *A Sort of Life* (New York: Simon & Schuster,

1971), 178. A similar account of and response to the General Strike can be found in Eric Ambler's autobiography, *Here Lies* (London: Weidenfeld & Nicolson, 1985), 69–71.

4   Licensed to look

1   Christopher Booker, *The Neophiliacs: A Study in the Revolution in English Life in the 1950s and 1960s* (London: Collins, 1969), 179.
2   Tony Bennett, 'James Bond as Popular Hero,' *U203 Popular Culture: Unit 21* (Milton Keynes: Open University Press, 1982), 6; John Sutherland, *Fiction and the Fiction Industry* (London: Athlone Press, 1978), 176.
3   Kingsley Amis, *The James Bond Dossier* (New York: New American Library, 1965), 111.
4   Julian Symons, *Bloody Murder* (Harmondsworth: Penguin, 1974), 246.
5   Quoted in Bennett, 'James Bond as Popular Hero,' 18.
6   Ian Fleming, *From Russia, With Love* (St Albans: Triad Panther, 1977), 47, 40.
7   Fleming, *From Russia With Love*, 87–8, 123.
8   Ian Fleming, *The Man With the Golden Gun* (New York: New American Library, 1966), 157.
9   Ian Fleming, *The Spy Who Loved Me* (London: Pan Books, 1967), 118.
10   Umberto Eco, 'Narrative Structures in Fleming,' in *The Role of the Reader* (Bloomington: Indiana University Press, 1979).
11   Fleming, *From Russia, With Love*, 169, 170.
12   Ian Fleming, *Moonraker* (London: Pan Books, 1956), 19; Ian Fleming, *Goldfinger* (London: Pan Books, 1961), 90.
13   Bennett, 'James Bond as Popular Hero,' 18–20.
14   Fleming, *From Russia, With Love*, 98–9.
15   Louis Turner and John Ash, *The Golden Hordes: International Tourism and the Pleasure Periphery* (London: Constable, 1975).
16   Fleming, *From Russia, With Love*, 126.
17   Ian Fleming, *Dr. No* (London: Pan Books, 1960), 5–6.
18   Ian Fleming, *Live and Let Die* (London: Pan Books, 1957), 41, 50.
19   Bennett, 'James Bond as Popular Hero,' 13–14; Fleming, *Goldfinger*, 189; Ian Fleming, *Casino Royale* (London: Pan Books, 1955), 33.
20   Annette Kuhn, *Women's Pictures: Feminism and Cinema* (London: Routledge & Kegan Paul, 1982), 113; Laura Mulvey, 'Visual Pleasure and Narrative Cinema,' *Screen* 16 (1975): 6–18; Kuhn, *Women's Pictures*, 115.
21   Fleming, *Dr. No*, 67.

22 Fleming, *From Russia, With Love*, 131, 139–40.
23 Fleming, *From Russia, With Love*, 149–50.
24 Herbert Marcuse, *One-Dimensional Man* (Boston: Beacon Press, 1964).
25 A good deal of contemporary cultural history and analysis is condensed in this account: see in particular the work of Janice Winship: 'Advertising in Women's Magazines, 1956–1974,' Centre for Contemporary Cultural Studies Occasional Paper No.59 (1980); 'Woman Becomes an Individual: Femininity and Consumption in Women's Magazines, 1954–1969,' Centre for Contemporary Cultural Studies Occasional Paper No.65 (1981); 'Sexuality for Sale,' in S. Hall and others, *Culture, Language, Media* (London: Hutchinson, 1980); 'A Woman's World,' in Women's Studies Group, *Women Take Issue* (London: Hutchinson, 1978); Barbara Ehrenreich, *The Hearts of Men* (London: Pluto Press, 1983); and Rosalind Coward, ' "Sexual liberation" and the family,' *m/f* 1 (1978): 7–24.

5 Looking-glass wars

1 Ian Fleming, *From Russia, With Love* (St Albans: Triad Panther, 1977), 189, 199.
2 Quoted in Tony Bennett, 'James Bond as Popular Hero,' *U203 Popular Culture: Unit 21* (Milton Keynes: Open University Press, 1982), 10–11.
3 See, for example, Ronald A. Knox, 'Detective Story Decalogue,' in H. Haycraft (ed.), *The Art of the Mystery Story* (New York: Simon & Schuster, 1946).
4 LeRoy Panek, *The Special Branch* (Bowling Green, Ohio: Bowling Green University Popular Press, 1981), 220.
5 John Sutherland, *Fiction and the Fiction Industry* (London: Athlone Press, 1978), 60.
6 Graham Greene, *The Human Factor* (New York: Avon Books, 1979), 42; Marie-Françoise Allain, *The Other Man: Conversations with Graham Greene* (New York: Simon & Schuster, 1983), 148; Greene, *The Human Factor*, 125.
7 The details of Philby's career come from: Kim Philby, *My Silent War* (St Albans: Panther, 1969); B. Page, D. Leitch and P. Knightley, *Philby: The Spy Who Betrayed a Generation* (London: Sphere Books, 1977); P. Seale and M. McConville, *Philby: The Long Road to Moscow* (Harmondsworth: Penguin, 1978); and Andrew Boyle, *The Climate of Treason* (London: Coronet, 1980).
8 John le Carré, Introduction, to Page and others, *Philby*, 31, 27.

9   Hugh Thomas (ed.), *The Establishment* (London: New English Library, 1962), 18, 13–14.

10   Raymond Williams, *Culture and Society, 1780—1950* (New York: Harper & Row, 1966), 329.

11   Andrew Gamble, *Britain in Decline* (London: Macmillan, 1981), 123.

12   Graham Greene, *Ways of Escape* (New York: Pocket Books, 1980), 267–8.

13   John le Carré, *Tinker, Tailor, Soldier, Spy* (New York: Bantam Books, 1975), 367. On Malcolm Muggeridge's view of Philby's fascist sympathies, see Malcolm Muggeridge, 'Refractions in the Character of Kim Philby,' in his *Things Past* (London: Collins, 1978); Page and others, *Philby*, 24; and Boyle, *The Climate of Treason*, 145.

14   Graham Greene, *Collected Essays* (Harmondsworth: Penguin, 1970), 311.

15   Le Carré, Introduction, 28.

16   'The rectangle is the representation of a binary opposition (two contraries), along with the simple negations (or contradictories) of both terms . . ., plus the various possible combinations of these terms.' Basically this device forces us to see 'that concepts do not exist in isolation but are defined in opposition to each other, in relatively organized clusters.' Fredric Jameson, *Fables of Aggression: Wyndham Lewis, the Modernist as Fascist* (Berkeley: University of California Press, 1979), 99; Fredric Jameson, 'After Armageddon: Character Systems in *Dr. Bloodmoney*,' *Science Fiction Studies* 2 (1975):42.

17   Umberto Eco, 'Narrative Structures in Fleming,' in *The Role of the Reader* (Bloomington: Indiana University Press, 1979); Jameson, 'After Armageddon.'

18   For example: 'The espionage and intrigue story is a contest of Good and Evil, with the Good winning out in its curious way: the more brutal the Evil, the more danger of provoking a crushing response from the Good': Robert Gillespie, 'The Recent Future: Secret Agents and the Cold War,' *Salmagundi* 13 (Summer 1970): 45–60; 'In the case of the thriller, the primary world is the soul's perpetual struggle between good and evil': Ralph Harper, *The World of the Thriller* (Baltimore: Johns Hopkins University Press, 1974), 17; 'the espionage thriller [with its] cumbersome theological apparatus of a dialectic of Good and Evil': Jameson, 'Class and Allegory in Contemporary Mass Culture: *Dog Day Afternoon* as a Political Film,' *Screen Education*, no.30 (Spring 1979):86.

19   Jameson, *Fables of Aggression*, 149.

20 Le Carré, *Tinker, Tailor, Soldier, Spy*, 132, 131, 355.
21 Greene, *The Human Factor*, 131.
22 Le Carré, Introduction, 28.
23 Le Carré, *Tinker, Tailor, Soldier, Spy*, 112–13.
24 Greene, *Ways of Escape*, 266.
25 Andrew Tolson, *The Limits of Masculinity* (New York: Harper & Row, 1977), 13.
26 Le Carré, *Tinker, Tailor, Soldier, Spy*, 364.
27 Le Carré, *Tinker, Tailor, Soldier, Spy*, 368, 346, 347, 345.
28 Le Carré, *Tinker, Tailor, Soldier, Spy*, 74.
29 Le Carré, *Tinker, Tailor, Soldier, Spy*, 162.
30 Greene, *The Human Factor*, 12, 155, 211.
31 Greene, *The Human Factor*, 243.
32 Le Carré, *Tinker, Tailor, Soldier, Spy*, 217, 309; Greene, *The Human Factor*, 128.
33 A.J. Greimas, 'The Cognitive Dimension of Narrative Discourse,' *New Literary History* 7 (1976):433–47.
34 Le Carré, *Tinker, Tailor, Solider, Spy*, 324.
35 Nicos Poulantzas, *Classes in Contemporary Capitalism* (London: New Left Books, 1975), 275; Desmond Bagley, *Running Blind* (London: Fontana, 1979), 7; Harry Braverman, *Labor and Monopoly Capital* (New York: Monthly Review Press, 1974), 82.
36 Greene, *The Human Factor*, 129, 36–7.
37 John le Carré, *The Looking-Glass War* (London: Pan Books, 1966), 229.
38 John le Carré, *The Honourable Schoolboy* (London: Pan Books, 1978), 497, 543.
39 Robert McCrum, *In the Secret State* (New York: Avon Books, 1980), 229.
40 E.P. Thompson, *Writing by Candlelight* (London: Merlin Press, 1980), 150.

Conclusion

1 Julian Symons, *Bloody Murder* (Harmondsworth: Penguin, 1974), 250.
2 John le Carré, *Tinker, Tailor, Soldier, Spy* (New York: Bantam Books, 1975), 355; John le Carré, Introduction, to B. Page, D. Leitsch and P. Knightley, *Philby: The Spy Who Betrayed a Generation* (London: Sphere Books, 1977), 33.
3 Jerry Palmer, *Thrillers: Genesis and Structure of a Popular Genre* (London: Edward Arnold, 1978), 211f.
4 John Sutherland, *Bestsellers* (London: Routledge & Kegan Paul, 1981), 173.

5   E.P. Thompson, *Writing by Candlelight* (London: Merlin Press, 1980), 131–2.

6   Sutherland, *Bestsellers*, 96.

7   For interesting accounts of the popular literature and memory of the Second World War, see Sutherland, *Bestsellers*; Ken Worpole, *Dockers and Detectives* (London: Verso, 1983); Richard Johnson and others, *Making Histories* (London: Hutchinson, 1982).

8   George Orwell, 'Boys' Weeklies,' in *The Collected Essays, Journalism, and Letters*, Volume 1 (London: Secker & Warburg, 1968), 484.

9   Ivan Ruff, *The Dark Red Star* (London: Pluto Press, 1985); Chris Mullin, *A Very British Coup* (London: Hodder & Stoughton, 1982); Raymond Williams, *The Volunteers* (London: Eyre Methuen, 1978).

10   Mullin, *A Very British Coup*, 150.

11   Raymond Williams, *Politics and Letters* (London: New Left Books, 1979), 297.

12   Le Carré, *Tinker, Tailor, Soldier, Spy*, 76.

13   Graham Greene, *The Human Factor* (New York: Avon Books, 1979), 61.

Index